Tasmania

WORLD BIBLIOGRAPHICAL SERIES

General Editors:
Robert G. Neville (Executive Editor)
John J. Horton

Robert A. Myers
Ian Wallace

Hans H. Wellisch
Ralph Lee Woodward, Jr.

John J. Horton is Deputy Librarian of the University of Bradford and was formerly Chairman of its Academic Board of Studies in Social Sciences. He has maintained a longstanding interest in the discipline of area studies and its associated bibliographical problems, with special reference to European Studies. In particular he has published in the field of Icelandic and of Yugoslav studies, including the two relevant volumes in the World Bibliographical Series.

Robert A. Myers is Associate Professor of Anthropology in the Division of Social Sciences and Director of Study Abroad Programs at Alfred University, Alfred, New York. He has studied post-colonial island nations of the Caribbean and has spent two years in Nigeria on a Fulbright Lectureship. His interests include international public health, historical anthropology and developing societies. In addition to *Amerindians of the Lesser Antilles: a bibliography* (1981), *A Resource Guide to Dominica, 1493-1986* (1987) and numerous articles, he has compiled the World Bibliographical Series volumes on *Dominica* (1987), *Nigeria* (1989) and *Ghana* (1991).

Ian Wallace is Professor of German at the University of Bath. A graduate of Oxford in French and German, he also studied in Tübingen, Heidelberg and Lausanne before taking teaching posts at universities in the USA, Scotland and England. He specializes in contemporary German affairs, especially literature and culture, on which he has published numerous articles and books. In 1979 he founded the journal *GDR Monitor*, which he continues to edit under its new title *German Monitor*.

Hans H. Wellisch is Professor emeritus at the College of Library and Information Services, University of Maryland. He was President of the American Society of Indexers and was a member of the International Federation for Documentation. He is the author of numerous articles and several books on indexing and abstracting, and has published *The Conversion of Scripts and Indexing and Abstracting: an International Bibliography*, and *Indexing from A to Z*. He also contributes frequently to *Journal of the American Society for Information Science*, *The Indexer* and other professional journals.

Ralph Lee Woodward, Jr. is Professor of History at Tulane University, New Orleans. He is the author of *Central America, a Nation Divided*, 2nd ed. (1985), as well as several monographs and more than seventy scholarly articles on modern Latin America. He has also compiled volumes in the World Bibliographical Series on *Belize* (1980), *El Salvador* (1988), *Guatemala* (Rev. Ed.) (1992) and *Nicaragua* (Rev. Ed.) (1994). Dr. Woodward edited the Central American section of the *Research Guide to Central America and the Caribbean* (1985) and is currently associate editor of Scribner's *Encyclopedia of Latin American History*.

VOLUME 194

Tasmania

I. Kepars

Compiler

CLIO PRESS
OXFORD, ENGLAND · SANTA BARBARA, CALIFORNIA
DENVER, COLORADO

British Library Cataloguing in Publication Data

I. Kepars
Tasmania. – (World bibliographical series; v. 194)
1. Tasmania – Bibliography
I. Title
016.9′946

ISBN 1–85109–273–0

ABC-CLIO Ltd.,
Old Clarendon Ironworks,
35A Great Clarendon Street,
Oxford OX2 6AT, England.

────────

ABC-CLIO Inc.,
130 Cremona Drive,
Santa Barbara,
CA 93116, USA.

Designed by Bernard Crossland.
Typeset by Columns Design Ltd., Reading, England.
Printed and bound in Great Britain by Bookcraft (Bath) Ltd., Midsomer Norton.

THE WORLD BIBLIOGRAPHICAL SERIES

This series, which is principally designed for the English speaker, will eventually cover every country (and many of the world's principal regions), each in a separate volume comprising annotated entries on works dealing with its history, geography, economy and politics; and with its people, their culture, customs, religion and social organization. Attention will also be paid to current living conditions – housing, education, newspapers, clothing, etc.– that are all too often ignored in standard bibliographies; and to those particular aspects relevant to individual countries. Each volume seeks to achieve, by use of careful selectivity and critical assessment of the literature, an expression of the country and an appreciation of its nature and national aspirations, to guide the reader towards an understanding of its importance. The keynote of the series is to provide, in a uniform format, an interpretation of each country that will express its culture, its place in the world, and the qualities and background that make it unique. The views expressed in individual volumes, however, are not necessarily those of the publisher.

VOLUMES IN THE SERIES

Contents

Contents

Contents

Introduction

Geography

Tasmania, Australia's smallest state, consists of a group of islands lying south of the south-east corner of the Australian mainland, separated from it by the Bass Strait which is approximately 240 kilometres wide. It covers an area of 68,331 square kilometres, of which the main island occupies 64,409. Macquarie Island, a part of the state, lies in the Southern Ocean, approximately 1300 kilometres south-east of Tasmania. The Tasmanian mainland extends just 296 kilometres from north to south and 315 kilometres from east to west. It is about the size of Switzerland or Scotland, but just under one-third of the size of Victoria, the smallest of Australia's mainland states.

Tasmania is one of the most mountainous islands in the world, but few peaks exceed 1500 metres – the highest being Mt. Ossa at 1617 metres. A substantial part of the Central Plateau is also above 900 metres. Tasmania is distinguished from mainland Australia by the great number of freshwater lakes, mainly situated on the Central Plateau, and by its permanently running rivers.

The climate is classifed as temperate maritime and, unlike mainland Australia, there is reliable all-year-round rainfall. Being south of latitude 40°, Tasmania is on the edge of the Roaring Forties and, with South America being the nearest land mass to the west, the island's weather is subject at times to strong winds and heavy rain in the south and west coastal areas.

Only occasionally, Tasmania experiences the hot temperatures common in the mainland Australian states. Typical daily maximum temperatures during summer are from 17 to 26°C, while normal winter minimums range from about 0 to 6°C.

Until the last ice age some 12,000 years ago, Tasmania was linked to mainland Australia by a land-bridge used by Aborigines and animals. When the seas rose and created Bass Strait, the subsequent isolation led to the development of unique animals and plants. Tasmania's fauna includes representatives of the three main groups of mammals: placentals, monotremes and marsupials. The carnivorous Tasmanian devil, the Tasmanian tiger or thylacine (probably extinct) and the long-tailed mouse, are among those which are unique to Tasmania. An important feature of the mammal fauna is the relative abundance of some species: the potoroo, bettong, eastern barred bandicoot and the quolls are quite common, whereas they are severely depleted or extinct on the mainland. Of the 220 or so recorded species of birds, 13 are endemic.

Because of its geographical isolation, Tasmania today has one of the world's last unspoiled temperate rainforests, which is a haven for its endemic plant species, of which there are about 300.

In order to preserve this unique wilderness, about 1,383,600 hectares (20 per cent of the state) has been declared the Tasmanian Wilderness World Heritage Area and inscribed on the World Heritage list by the World Heritage Committee of UNESCO. The World Heritage Area contains rare and ancient plants, tall eucalyptus forests, distinctive and unique animals, important alpine and sub-alpine areas, glacial features and magnificent scenery. There are also extensive cave systems and sites of Aboriginal as well as European cultural significance.

All this unspolt wilderness and dramatic scenery makes Tasmania an ideal holiday destination, especially for the tourist interested in outdoor activities, such as hiking, canoeing or fishing. Since the introduction of trout in 1864, Tasmania with its many lakes and rivers has been an angler's paradise, especially for the fly-fishing enthusiast. The gourmet is also well served, as Tasmania is noted for its excellent fruit and vegetables, cheese, seafood and, increasingly, for its wines. There are many excellent restaurants on the island. Historic buildings, dating to the colonial years of the 19th century and often lovingly restored, also attract the visitor. An excellent road system gives easy access to the major lakes, rivers and estuaries, as well as to the fringes of the wilderness.

Population

The resident population of Tasmania in 1995 was 473,000. It was the fifth consecutive year to record markedly declining population growth. During the year Tasmania's population increased by only 558 persons or 0.12 per cent, which was about one-tenth of Australia's rate of 1.21 per cent growth for the same period. The declining population growth resulted from an increasingly negative net interstate migration of 2715 persons. Because of an unpredictable economy and conservative social environment, escape to mainland Australia by the younger generation in order find better job prospects and intellectual stimulation, has always been Tasmania's demographic reality. Unlike mainland Australia, Tasmania is not dominated by a single metropolis, the urban population being divided between two large towns: the capital Hobart (with about 194,000 inhabitants) in the south and Launceston in the north, and several smaller towns. Because of the reliable rainfall the population is much more evenly spread than in the rest of Australia, a higher percentage (about 25 per cent) living in rural areas than in any other state of Australia. The descendants of the Aborignes represent around 1.5 per cent of the total population. As a result of Australia's post-war immigration programmes, there are representatives of every ethnic community in Tasmania, but there are far fewer transcontinental migrants, especially from Asia. Less than 1 per cent of immigrants intend to settle in the island state.

History

The first settlers, the Aborigines, came to Tasmania probably some 20,000 years ago when the island was still connected to the mainland. It is estimated that there were about 3000 to 4000 Aborigines when the first Europeans – the French – encountered them. They were mainly scattered along the coast in separate tribes, and spoke several languages. When the English colonizers arrived in 1804, a long series of fatal encounters began, culminating in the extermination of most full-blood Aborigines in a single generation. Between 1830 and 1834, all Aborigines still alive were rounded up and settled on Flinders Island in Bass Strait 'for their own protection'. Their numbers continued to dwindle and the few who remained were moved back to Oyster Cove, south of Hobart. The last full-blood male died in 1869 and Truganini, once the wife of a chief but by this time the last of her race, died in 1876. The destruction of the Aborigines is a dark page in Tasmania's history and for a century was a taboo subject, until the reassessment by historians during the 1970s and 1980s of the early settlement of Australia. It was realized that the colonization of Australia was accompanied by violence and dispossession. This awareness led to the recognition that Tasmania still has a significant Aboriginal population, albeit of mixed blood.

The Dutch navigator Abel Tasman discovered Tasmania in 1642 and named it Van Diemen's Land. For 130 years there was no exploration, but both the French and the English probed the coastline from 1772 onwards. To forestall the French and in order to develop sealing, Tasmania was formally claimed for the British and in 1803 the first settlement was established on the eastern shore of the River Derwent at Risdon Cove. The total number of the party was 49, including 35 convicts. In 1804, a further 262 persons arrived, including 178 convicts, under Colonel David Collins. He established a settlement at Sullivan Cove, the present site of Hobart, and named it 'Hobart Town', the name which remained in official use until 1881, when it was shortened to Hobart.

During the first few years both settlements struggled for survival, but by the early 1820s, both wool and wheat were being exported and free settlers prospered thanks to a system of generous land grants and cheap convict labour. In 1820 it was estimated that the population was 5468, of whom 2588 had arrived as convicts. After having been part of New South Wales since its foundation, Tasmania became a separate colony in 1825. During the 1820s the population increased rapidly from 5468 to 24,279, including several thousands of free immigrants. However, the rate of arrival of convicts was even greater. Tasmania had the reputation of being the harshest of the British penal settlements. Conditions at the notorious convict settlement at Sarah Island in Macquarie Harbour on the west coast are well portrayed in Marcus Clarke's famous 19th-century novel, *For the term of his natural life*. The settlement was abandoned in the 1830s, when Port Arthur was established as the main penal settlement. By 1848 Van Diemen's Land was the only place in the British Empire for the transportation of convicts, and a strong anti-transportation movement advocated its abandonment. The last shipload of convicts arrived in 1853. Representative government was achieved soon afterwards, and the first elections took place in 1856. In 1855 the name Van Diemen's Land was officially changed to Tasmania, as if to erase the stain of the convict past. Throughout its history, and even today, Tasmanian society has been uncomfortable with its penal heritage. Port Arthur, which has become an important tourist destination, seemed to revert to its dark past in April 1996, when a lone gunman shot dead 35 and injured 18 tourists in the biggest mass murder in Australia's history.

On attaining self-government, the colony experienced an economic depression. From 1851 there was a steady exodus of Tasmanians to the newly discovered Victorian gold-fields. From 1858 to 1872 the population decreased and standards of living declined, but by the 1880s Tasmania had another boom in the west: the discovery of tin at Mount Bischoff marked the beginning of a new basic industry – mining. Subsequent finds of silver, gold and copper boosted the colony's economy. The drift of people to the mainland was reversed and the latter part of the century saw the population increase by over 80 per cent.

Federation of the Australian colonies arrived in 1901 and Tasmania officially became a state of the new Commonwealth of Australia, although a strong sense of regionalism prevails up to the present day. Mainlanders are regarded with suspicion and the state government in Hobart is forever at loggerheads with its federal counterparts in Canberra.

During the 20th century, Tasmania has grown rapidly. In the 1990s it has had the highest unemployment level of any Australian state. The rate has been consistently over 10 per cent, and peaked at 12.9 per cent in 1993. Furthermore, Tasmania's trade, like that of Australia, is vulnerable to world commodity prices. Any fluctuation in these, or in the value of the Australian dollar, the US dollar or the Japanese yen, influences the economic wellbeing of the Tasmanian population.

Mainly due to the incentive of cheap hydro-electric power, achieved by damming Tasmania's many wild rivers, some major industries have been established in the state. Cadbury Schweppes is the largest cocoa and confectionery factory in Australia, employing about 1000 people. Because of the favourable climate, there are other important companies processing agricultural and other produce: frozen vegetables, fruit, salmon, trout, lobsters and cheese being chief among them. Wood and paper products are significant industries. Australian Newsprint Mills is Australia's only producer of newsprint and supplies 60 per cent of Australia's requirement. Australia's first aluminium smelter, operated by Comalco Aluminium, was established at George Town in 1955. Pasminco Metals-EZ, is the largest producer of zinc in Australia, and one of the six top electrolytic zinc plants in the world. Air transport and shipping play a vital role in maintaining and developing passenger and freight flows between Tasmania and the mainland.

The Hydro-Electric Commission (HEC), established in the early years of the century, has the statutory responsibility to generate, transmit, distribute and sell electricity. Today it is the largest employer in the state with some 1700 employees and an annual income of nearly $500 million. Since its establishment it has dominated the state's political, industrial and economic policies. In the island state, blessed by an abundance of water, governments of all persuasions, influenced by the notion of progress as man's mastery over nature, have acquiesced to the HEC's enthusiasm for unlimited development of yet more power schemes. Only since the inundation of the beautiful alpine Lake Pedder to form the Serpentine Dam in the early 1970s, has the HEC become the focus of a heated debate about its undemocratic, behind-the-scenes influence on industrial development in Tasmania.

Introduction

Although criticism had been heard as long ago as the 1880s about Tasmania's over-exploitation of its timber resources, the Pedder hydro-electric scheme marshalled forces which, for the first time, challenged the ideology which had prevailed since 1804: advocating unfettered development without regard to the natural environment. The Tasmanian Green Movement was born, but fought a losing battle in the case of the flooding of Lake Pedder. However, the Greens were victorious in their fight to prevent the HEC's proposal to dam the Gordon River in the south-west, which would have flooded the Franklin, one of the last wild rivers in the world. In 1983, the High Court of Australia delcared the dam works illegal and, as a consequence of success in this struggle, the Green Party won a historic balance of power in the Tasmanian State Parliament in 1989. It failed soon afterwards, but the Greens have been winning Parliamentary seats in every subsequent election. Since then, Tasmanian politics have been marked by the conflict between the Greens and Tasmania's developers. Another victory for the conservationists has been the recent abandonment of a large export pulp mill at Wesley Vale on the north coast.

With its small population (under 500,000) Tasmania today is at a crossroads. Recent opinion seems to suggest that the future lies in the exploitation of its pristine (sic!) natural environment for tourism – already the largest employer – but entrenched conservatism still argues for 'development'. In a world calling for a cleaner, greener environment, the number of visitors every year already exceeds the population of the state. The clean environment is Tasmania's main attraction in the promotion of tourism.

About the bibliography

This bibliography directs the reader to books on all aspects of Tasmania and its people. The selection emphasizes sources which explain those aspects of Tasmania which, in the compiler's view, express its unique qualities and background. It is hoped that the works included will stimulate the reader's curiosity regarding Australia's island state, and so encourage further reading.

The book is intended for the informed general reader, as well as for the scholar who wishes to obtain background information in a field other than his own. It should be useful to both the short- and the long-term visitor and also intending migrants, or persons interested in transacting business in Tasmania. It will serve as a reference tool for librarians, booksellers and others who are frequently asked to recommend books in a particular subject area, and can be used as a selection tool by librarians wishing to assemble or develop a basic collection for Tasmanian studies.

The selection of suitable titles for inclusion in the bibliography was done in the National Library of Australia in Canberra. Being a legal deposit institution for Australian publications, it holds most of the books included in the bibliography. More than 95 per cent of the selections were examined by the compiler and, for the rest, reviews were used in exercising choice for inclusion.

The bibliography includes classic accounts, general surveys, thorough summaries and books which, for want of a better phrase, add 'local colour', and hopefully will kindle a spark of curosity in the reader to delve deeper and further. Such a keen reader will note that many of the listed titles contain extensive bibliographies or suggestions for further reading. He or she may also wish to consult the Tasmanian Historical Research Association's *Papers and Proceedings*, which in the first issue of each year lists all publications of Tasmanian interest published in the previous year.

Following the truism that 'a picture is worth a thousand words', pictorial works and those generously illustrated have an honoured place in the bibliography.

The monograph literature about Tasmania does not cover every aspect of the island and the life of its people adequately. Biographies, which throw light on the wider field of endeavour of the biographee, or which fill a gap in the literature in a particular field of knowledge, have been included within appropriate subject sections and they also appear under biographies in the index. Genealogical works are excluded. Selected works of fiction and poetry, when they illuminate some important aspect of Tasmania, are also included. As far as possible the arrangement of books within each section is hierarchical. The general introductions and surveys of the subject are followed by works of specialized interest and increasing complexity. The intended audience of a book is often indicated in the annotation. The map has been reproduced with the kind permission of the Land Information Bureau in Tasmania.

Although the emphasis of the bibliography is on books, the more important newspapers, periodicals and magazines in a variety of fields are listed. Periodical articles may be accessed through APAIS: Australian Public Affairs Information Service. It is accumulated annually and should be available in large libraries overseas. Beginning in 1997, the National Library of Australia will be introducing the World 1 Service, an integrated information resource of document descriptions and location information. The service will search across all physical forms in which information is held. A keyword search will provide a result that includes descriptions of books, journal articles, photographs, etc. World 1 will be available on a user's PC through the Internet anywhere in the world.

Throughout this bibliography the emphasis is on recent publications, some of which may be available from specialist bookshops in English-speaking countries, but intending purchasers may be more successful writing directly to the publishers. Older works, as well as more recent ones which are out of print, should be available on interlibrary loan from national or university libraries, especially those that have some involvement with Australian studies. When World 1 is up and running, users will be able to obtain the document by ordering a fax or by placing an interlibrary loan request. A full text document will be available for viewing directly on a PC or as a printout.

I am grateful for the assistance given to me by Maija Kepars who unselfishly acted the part of the informed general reader by critically commenting on the language, content and general comprehensibility of the annotations which describe each entry in the bibliography.

The Island and Its People

1   **The quiet land.**
    Photographs by Peter Dombrovskis. Text by Ellen Miller, with an
    introduction by Nick Evers.   Hobart: Peter Dombrovskis, 1977. 111p.
An evocation of Tasmania through the photographs of Dombrovskis and Miller's
prose-poems which weave between the photographs. The introductory essay explores
the notion of Tasmania's 'spirit' and presents a personal interpretation of the meaning
of wilderness to urban man.

2   **The Tasmania we love.**
    Ruth Park, Cedric Emmanuel.   Melbourne: Nelson, 1987. 120p.
A collaboration between Ruth Park, a well-known author, and Cedric Emmanuel who
is a landscape artist. In words, paintings and drawings they combine to capture the
spirit of the island state of Australia.

3   **Tasmania's heritage: an enduring legacy.**
    Jennifer Pringle-Jones, Ray Joyce.   Hobart: St David's Park Publishing,
    1991. 144p.
Tasmania's heritage is explored in numerous coloured photographs, with accompanying text. There are eight chapters: Heritage of nature; Settlement; Exploration; The
sea; Contribution of convicts; Architecture; Industry and commerce; The arts and
leisure. The book is an excellent introduction to the island for the intending tourist or
for the armchair traveller.

4   **Tasmania.**
    S. W. Jackman.   Melbourne: Wren Publishing, 1974. 200p. bibliog.
Published in *The Island Series*, this is a scholarly introduction to all aspects of
Australia's island state. The book was written during the author's extended stay as
visiting professor at the University of Tasmania.

1

5   **Down home: revisiting Tasmania.**
   Peter Conrad.   London: Chatto & Windus, 1988. 232p. maps.

Peter Conrad left Tasmania in 1968 and became a well-known academic and critic in Britain. After two decades he returned to his birthplace and rediscovered the island. The result is a fabulous book combining travel, autobiography and history – a must for anyone with an interest in Australia's island state.

6   **Crossing the gap: a novelist's essays.**
   C. J. Koch.   Sydney: Angus & Robertson, 1987. 167p.

Essays by the Tasmanian-born novelist Christopher Koch whose *The boys in the island* and *The doubleman* are set in Tasmania (see item no. 442). See especially the two essays 'Return to Hobart Town' and 'A Tasmanian note'.

7   **Handbook for Tasmania.**
   Edited by Leonard Cerutty.   Hobart: Government Printer, 1949. 127p.

Prepared for the 27th meeting of the Australian and New Zealand Association for the Advancement of Science held in Hobart in 1949. Written by authorities in their respective fields, this is a good general introduction to immediate post-war Tasmania covering the natural environment, industries and society.

Geography

General

8   **Tasmania.**
R. J. Solomon.   Sydney: Angus & Robertson, 1972. 95p. maps.
Produced in the series Australian Regional Geographies, which covers the major
physical and cultural aspects of the geography of Australia, Solomon here gives an
authoritative and informative description of the landscape, natural resources and
potential for economic development. The author is a professional geographer.

9   **Bass Strait: Australia's last frontier.**
Edited by Stephen Murray-Smith.   Sydney: Australian Broadcasting
Corporation, 1987. Rev. ed. 126p. bibliogs.
Bass Strait is the body of water which separates Tasmania from mainland Australia. It
contains over 100 islands which are mostly part of Tasmania, the largest two –
Flinders Island and King Island – are respectively 1374 sq km and 1099 sq km in area.
The book was first published in 1969 after the Australian Broadcasting Commission
commissioned a series of talks on Bass Strait. This revised and updated edition
contains chapters by experts in their fields on the Strait's history, geology, wildlife,
fishing, farming, prehistory, oil searches and scientific investigations.

10   **The climates of Tasmania.**
In: *Australian climate patterns.*   J. Gentilli.   Melbourne: Nelson,
1972, p. 248-259.
Chapter 16 surveys the climate of Tasmania.

3

11 **Geology and mineral resources of Tasmania.**
Edited by C. F. Burrett, E. L. Martin. Brisbane: Geological Society of
Australia, 1989. 574p. maps. bibliog. (Special Publication, no. 15).

Published for the Australian Bicentennial in 1988 and in commemoration of the
publication of R. M. Johnston's pioneering volume *A systematic account of the
geology of Tasmania* in 1888, this work is the latest word on the geology of Tasmania.
A detailed bibliography of 44 pages completes the book.

12 **The mountains of northeastern Tasmania: a study of alpine
geomorphology.**
Nel Caine. Rotterdam: Balkema, 1983. 200p. maps. bibliog.

A scientific study of alpine geomorphology in the mountains of northeastern Tasmania.
The text is accessible only to specialist scholars.

Maps and atlases

13 **Holiday atlas of Tasmania.**
Hobart: Tasmap.

Published irregularly, this handy 30-page (1986 edition) atlas is indispensable for the
tourist visting Tasmania. Contains road maps of the island and street maps of all the
large towns, pointing out the locations of accommodation and tourist attractions. It
also offers excellent summaries of attractions in the various tourist regions.

14 **Atlas of Tasmania.**
Edited by J. L. Davies. Hobart: Lands and Surveys Department, 1965. 128p.

Now 30 years old and out-of-date in its presentation of statistics of human occupation
and land use, the atlas is still very useful for the collocation of geographical
information on Tasmania.

15 **The printed maps of Tasmania 1642-1900.**
R. V. Tooley. London: The Map Collectors Circle, 1975.
88p. + 49 plates. (Map Collectors Series, no. 5).

This 1975 edition is much more comprehensive – although still not a complete listing
of the maps of Tasmania – than the 1963 edition. Tooley's larger work *The mapping
of Australia*, published in 1979, incorporates the 1975 edition as a chapter.

16 **Guide to maps in the Tasmanian Parliamentary papers 1856-1981.**
J. McQuilton, J. MacCulloch. Introduction by R. Kellaway. Sydney:
School of History, University of New South Wales, 1986. 59p.

Maps are listed in chronological order. The index is divided into two parts: a subject
index and a place-names index. Roger Kellaway has written an extremely clear and
useful introductory essay on the use of the Tasmanian Parliamentary papers which is a
boon to any researcher in the island's history.

Discovery and Exploration

17   **The discovery of Tasmania.**
     H. G. Taylor.   Hobart: Cat & Fiddle Press, 1973. 177p.
A chronological account of thirteen voyages of discovery to or around Tasmania by
Dutch, English and French navigators, starting with Tasman in 1642 and ending with
Nicolas Baudin's expedition, 1800-1804. Although acknowledgement is made to the
State Library of Tasmania, the Mitchell Library in Sydney and the Alexander Turnbull
Library in New Zealand, no bibliography is provided, but there is an excellent index.

18   **The early history of Tasmania: the geographical era 1642-1804.**
     R. W. Giblin.   London: Methuen, 1928. 341p. maps. bibliog.
A detailed account of the age of discovery and maritime exploration of Tasmania.
There are reproductions of the original explorers' charts and maps. The book is also
useful for the understanding of early European–Aboriginal contacts and race relations.

19   **The discovery of Tasmania: journal extracts from the expeditions
     of Abel Janszoon Tasman and Marc-Joseph Marion Dufresne
     1642-1772.**
     Edited by Edward Duyker. Translated by Edward, Herman and Maryse
     Duyker.   Hobart: St David's Park Publishing, 1992. 106p. maps.
     bibliog.
The editor states in the introduction: 'This anthology aims to bring together in one
volume, transcriptions and English translations of journal extracts (excluding naviga-
tional logs) from the first two European expeditions to Tasmania, an island which
entered the European imagination three and a half centuries ago with the voyage of the
Dutch explorer Abel Janszoon Tasman (circa 1603-1659). Besides the introduction
there is also a section of biographical notes about the main personalities and an up-to-
date bibliography. Another translation of Tasman's journal was published in 1942 to
celebrate the 300th anniversary of the discovery of Tasmania – *The discovery of
Tasmania 1642: selections from Doctor J. E. Heeres translation of Tasman's journal
Aug.-Dec. 1642.*

20 **The French exploration of Australia: with special reference to Tasmania.**
L. A. Triebel, J. C. Batt.   Hobart: L. G. Shea, Government Printer, 1957. 94p. maps. bibliog.
An outline history of the French contributions to the exploration of Tasmania and Australia.

21 **The general: the visits of the expedition led by Bruni d'Entrecasteaux to Tasmanian waters in 1792 and 1793.**
Brian Plomley, Josiane Piard-Bernier.   Launceston: Queen Victoria Museum, 1993. 379p. maps. bibliog.
D'Entrecasteaux's expedition had two main objectives: to search for La Pérouse, who had disappeared after his expedition left Botany Bay in 1788, and to conduct scientific research. This book has little to say about the search for La Pérouse; instead it focuses on the daily activities aboard the two ships, the *Recherche* and the *Espérance*, the explorations made, the scientific work and the contacts with the Aborigines during the two visits to Van Diemen's Land.

22 **Explorers of western Tasmania.**
C. J. Binks.   Devonport: Taswegia, 1989. 263p. maps. bibliog.
First published in 1980, the book is now reprinted in a soft-cover second edition. It is the only comprehensive history of the exploration of one of the most impenetrable wilderness areas in Australia. The period covered is from 1815 to 1889. The text includes passages from explorers' diaries and is aided by a number of coloured plates, numerous black-and-white prints and more than 30 maps detailing the routes taken by the explorers.

23 **Tasmania a wild beauty: the traditional lore of the island's wilderness.**
Paddy Maclean. Photographs by Dennis Harding.   Launceston: Regal Publications, 1989. 128p.
By using accounts of past explorers and miscellaneous travellers, the book attempts to demonstrate how the discovery of the almost unbelievable beauty of the Tasmanian wilderness often overshadowed their primary objectives of opening new country for commercial purposes. Many coloured photographs of the wild country amply attest to its beauty.

24 **Backsight: a history of surveying in Tasmania.**
Alan Jones.   Hobart: The Institution of Surveyors, Australia.
Tasmanian Division, 1989. 236p. maps. bibliog.
The story of surveying in Tasmania from its foundation in 1803 to Federation in 1900. Surveying in new lands is inextricably linked to exploration and land settlement. Therefore, the book is recommended to those readers with an interest not only in surveying, but also in the early exploration, mapping and settlement of Tasmania.

25   **The diaries of John Helder Wedge 1824-1835.**
      Edited by Mr Justice Crawford, W. F. Ellis, G. H. Stancombe.   Hobart:
      The Royal Society of Tasmania, 1962. 99p. map. bibliog.

Wedge, who arrived in Van Diemen's Land in 1824, was a surveyor, explorer and pioneer pastoralist. These diaries about his explorations and survey work were originally sent to his father in England and give a graphic account of the labour and hardships endured on his many ventures into previously unexplored country.

Tourist and Travel Guides

Travel guides

26 **Tasmania.**
   Michael Cook.   Sydney: Little Hills Press, 1996. 2nd ed. 160p. maps.
An up-to-date, comprehensive guide for the traveller to Australia's most scenic state.

27 **Tasmania: walks, wildlife and wonderful food.**
   Libby Buhrich.   Sydney: Millenium Books, 1995. Rev. & updated ed.
   174p.
An essential companion for the discerning traveller, this guidebook covers planning
the trip, accommodation, restaurants, places of interest, walks, day tours, wildlife and
flora.

28 **The untourist guide to Tasmania.**
   Suzanne Baker.   Sydney: UnTourist Co., 1994. 151p. maps.
Intended for the discerning traveller who wants to avoid the 'touristy' places. The
book contains information about local accommodation, experiences and sights away
from the well-worn track. A full-colour map of Tasmania is included and there are
many illustrations.

29 **Tasmania – a guide.**
   Sally Farrell Odgers.   Sydney: Kangaroo Press, 1989. 224p. maps.
   bibliogs.
A detailed, traditional guide book to Tasmania for the tourist and visitor who want to
explore the island by car.

30 **Tasmania.**
   In: *Reader's Digest illustrated guide to Australian places.* Sydney:
   Reader's Digest, 1993, p. 634-669.
A guide to Tasmanian geographical places including cities and towns and natural landmarks. The places are entered in the guide under natural regions. Each region is shown on a detailed map. Each entry on a place contains a description of its history and other noteworthy features. There are many coloured photographs.

31 **Discovering King Island Western Bass Strait.**
   Jean Edgecombe.   Sydney: The Author, 1993. 152p. maps. bibliog.
At 1099 sq km, the second largest island in Bass Strait, King Island today is mainly a tourist destination. The local inhabitants engage in dairying and fishing and produce superb cheeses and seafood. The book is a guide for the tourist but also provides historical interludes. A history of the island, by long-time resident R. H. Hooper, is *The King Island story.* It came out in a second edition, edited by Dr Mark Richmond, in 1980.

32. **Flinders Island and Eastern Bass Strait.**
   Jean Edgecombe.   Sydney: Edgekirk, 1986. 159p. bibliog.
Flinders is the largest of the Tasmanian islands in Bass Strait. It comprises 1374 sq km. The book introduces the reader and potential visitor to Flinders Island as well as the numerous islands which make up the Furneaux Group of the north-east corner of Tasmania. For a personal account of life on Flinders, see *Latitude forty: reminiscences of Flinders Island.* It was written by Jim Davie who arrived on the island as a migrant from Britain in 1923.

33 **Tasmanian heritage directory.**
   Tasmanian Branch of the Museums Association of Australia.   Hobart:
   Museums Association of Australia, Tasmanian Branch, 1991. 135p.
   maps.
This directory is a comprehensive guide to all Tasmanian galleries, museums, historical society collections and heritage parks. Besides listing information on hours of opening, admission charges and location, the directory also contains descriptions of the buildings, their historical significance and comment on the locality. It would be very useful to the tourist interested to learn about Tasmania's heritage.

Description and travel

34 **The splendour of Tasmania.**
   Photography by Dennis Harding. Text by Roddy Maclean.
   Launceston: D. & L. Books, 1989. 128p.
A large-format book of colour photographs depicting the Tasmanian landscape.

35 **Tasmania: Australia's treasure.**
Hobart: Department of the Premier and Cabinet, 1985. 148p.

A large-format volume chiefly containing coloured photographs of the Tasmanian landscape and the activities of the island's inhabitants. There is a basic textual introduction.

36 **Vanishing Tasmania: a photographic essay.**
Frank Bolt. Hobart: Waratah Publications, 1992. 288p.

A professional photographer's black-and-white record of the surviving remains of Tasmania's past. Subjects covered include farms and rural industries, houses, gardens, villages, hotels, transport, churches, mining and the convict era. It is an excellent evocation of Tasmania's past as shown by the present. There is a short textual introduction to each section and each photograph is accompanied by an historical caption.

37 **Stones of a century.**
Michael Sharland, with illustrations by the author. Hobart: O.B.M., 1969. 2nd ed. 78p.

The author first published this landmark book in 1952 as a contribution towards the movement for the preservation of historic buildings and relics of Tasmanian settlement. Many of these are now listed in the Register of the National Estate. They are illustrated in black-and-white photographs taken by the author.

38 **Oddity and elegance.**
Michael Sharland, illustrations by the author. Hobart: Fullers Bookshop, 1966. 134p.

Sharland was a pioneer advocate for the preservation of Tasmania's historical heritage. In this volume, through text and photographs, he presents a selection of historical sites, buildings and landscapes which are suitable, in his opinion, for preservation.

39 **The heritage of Tasmania: the illustrated Register of the National Estate.**
Melbourne: Macmillan, in association with the Australian Heritage Commission, 1983. 160p. maps.

An exhaustive listing, by region, of all cultural heritage, historic sites and buildings as well as sites of importance to Aboriginal history in Tasmania, included in the Register of the National Estate. A detailed description accompanied by photographs of each item listed is included. This work draws on *The heritage of Australia: the illustrated Register of the National Estate* published in 1981. The present volume includes items added to the Register in the intervening years and is of a convenient size to be used as a glove-box guide by the tourist.

40 **Heart of the north.**
Photographs by Owen Hughes. Text by Sir Raymond Ferrall.
Launceston: Owen Hughes Photography, 1988. 128p.

A pictorial work of colour photographs of Launceston and the surrounding districts.

41   **Richard Bennett's Huon Valley: a photographic essay.**
      Richard Bennett.   Geeveston: Richard Bennett, 1988. 96p. map.
The book contains colour art photographs of the beautiful Huon River Valley south of
Hobart. Bennett, who is Huon born and bred, is a professional photographer.

42   **South west Tasmania.**
      Richard Bennett.   Hobart: Richard Bennett, 1991. 96p.
Bennett, a professional photographer, evokes the harsh beauty of Tasmania's south-
west wilderness in this photographic essay.

43   **Tasmanian photographer: from the John Watt Beattie collection.**
      Compiled by Margaret Tassell, David Wood.   Melbourne: Macmillan,
      1981. 156p. bibliog.
Beattie was a pioneer professional photographer, who became Photographer to the
Government of Tasmania in 1896. He contributed more than anyone at the time to the
development of the public's visual image of Tasmania. His photographs were used to
illustrate tourist guides, in newspaper pictorial feature articles and in public displays.
As a consequence of his wide travels through Tasmania's remote areas he was
publicly advocating the setting aside of specific areas for conservation purposes. The
photographs selected for the book come from the collections of the Queen Victoria
Museum and Art Gallery in Launceston.

44   **The Main Road: an historical journey from Launceston to Hobart.**
      G. J. O'Brien. Photographs by Jenny Dickens.   Launceston: Telegraph
      Printers, c. 1981. 90p.
Describes the 180-km journey from north to south along the Midlands Highway
connecting Tasmania's two largest cities. Useful for the tourist as it lists and describes
all sites of interest encountered on the drive. Added interest is provided by the
inclusion of passages of text about the journey by previous travellers, such as Anthony
Trollope, the novelist, in 1871, and James Backhouse, a renowned member of the
Society of Friends, in 1833.

45   **Tasmanian journey.**
      A. Geoffrey Horner.   Hobart: Cat & Fiddle Press, 1974. 128p.
'An informal travel book' written in 1936, but not published until 1974. Well written,
with historical insights, this book is interesting today for the attitudes it displays of the
1930s in Tasmania.

46   **Isle of mountains: roaming through Tasmania.**
      Charles Barrett.   Melbourne: Cassell, 1944. 263p.
This guidebook to Tasmania during World War II is characterized by the author's skill
in combining anecdotes with shrewd personal observations. It is still entertaining to
read today.

47 **Tasmania by road and track.**
E. T. Emmett. Melbourne: Melbourne University Press, 1952. 170p.

In this book, which resulted from the notes he made on an extensive walking tour of Tasmania, the author, a former Director of the Tasmanian Tourist Department, links landscape and history.

48 **Walk to the West.**
James Backhouse Walker. Edited for the Royal Society of Tasmania by D. Michael Stoddart. Hobart: Artemis Publishing Consultants, 1993. 76p. maps.

This lavish publication commemorates the 150th anniversary of the Royal Society of Tasmania. The journal, describing a walk to the west coast in early 1887 by a group drawn from Hobart's civic élite, is not remarkable in itself. The value of the book lies in the fine reproductions by the colonial landcape artist W. C. Piguenit of his western Tasmanian paintings, and Stoddart's scholarly introduction and annotations.

49 **Islands of Bass Strait.**
Text by Patsy Adam-Smith. Photographs by John Powell. Adelaide: Rigby, 1978. 56p.

An eyewitness account of life on the 42 islands of the Furneaux Group by the prolific author Patsy Adam-Smith. She has lived and worked with the people of the islands. This experience has helped her to capture the unique lifestyle of the islanders – descendants of sealers, abandoned seamen, escapees and abducted Aborigines from Tasmania. Many photographs add colour to the text.

50 **The Tasmanian traveller: a nineteenth century companion for modern travellers.**
Collected and edited by Hilary Webster. Canberra: Brolga Press, 1988. 192p.

A collection of diverse accounts of 19th-century travel in Tasmania which should be of interest to visitors to the island in providing background to their own travels.

Natural History

General

51 **Tracks of the morning: selected items from a naturalist's notebook.**
Michael Sharland ('Peregrine' of *The Mercury*).   Hobart: The Mercury,
1981. 144p.

Published by *The Mercury* (see item no. 511) to celebrate the 60th year of Sharland's
natural history contributions to the newspaper. Sharland's articles also range over
Tasmanian pioneering days and local folklore. A similar anthology of his writings was
published in 1971, entitled *A pocketful of nature*. Black-and-white photographs
accompany the text.

52 **South-west Tasmania: a natural history and visitors guide.**
Ken Collins.   Hobart: Heritage Books, 1990. 368p. maps. bibliog.

An excellent presentation of the geology, flora and fauna of the World Heritage
wilderness area in south-west Tasmania. Indispensable for anyone intending to
venture into the area. There are numerous colour photographs and useful maps for the
hiker in this lavish, pocket-size production.

53 **A naturalist in Tasmania.**
Geoffrey Smith.   Oxford: Clarendon Press, 1909. 147p.

This book resulted from a six-month sojourn in Tasmania by the author, a Fellow of
New College, Oxford, to study the freshwater life of the island. It is an interesting,
well-written account of his travels and observations around Tasmania at a time when
nature there was in a much wilder state than it is today.

54 **My home in Tasmania.**
Louisa Meredith.   Adelaide: Sullivan's Cove, 1979. 2nd ed. 221p.

First published in 1852 under the title *My home in Tasmania, during a residence of nine years*, this is an intelligent and perceptive description of the author's own experience of colonial society and the natural environment of Tasmania. Her observations are acute, vivid and lively. The book is one of the best contemporary accounts about early Tasmania, illustrated with the author's own black-and-white sketches. For readers interested in a closer study of a remarkable woman, Vivienne Rae-Ellis's *Louise Anne Meredith: a tigress in exile* (1979, and republished in 1990), is recommended.

55 **Islands of south-west Tasmania.**
Gary White.   Sydney: The Author, 1981. Enlarged ed. 79p. map.
bibliog.

A survey of the natural history of the small group of inhospitable islands off the south-west coast of Tasmania. They are exposed to the full force of the Roaring Forties and are uninhabited by man. Unique black-and-white photographs amply demonstrate the harsh environment of the islands.

56 **Sub-Antarctic sanctuary: summertime on Macquarie Island.**
Mary E. Gillham.   Sydney: Reed, 1967. 223p. maps. bibliog.

The botanist author was one of four pioneer women scientists, who spent a year in 1960 engaged in scientific investigations on Macquarie Island, as part of the Australian Antarctic Research Expedition for that year. This book presents a readable account of the natural history of the island. Isobel Bennett, a distinguished Australian marine biologist, was also a member of the team. She published *Shores of Macquarie Island* in 1972, also intended for the general reader. For a scientific survey of the natural history of Macquarie Island the interested reader may consult *Subantarctic Macquarie Island: environment and biology*, by P. M. Selkirk, R. D. Seppelt and D. R. Selkirk, in the Studies in Polar Research series, published by Cambridge University Press in 1990. Macquarie Island has been a wildlife sanctuary since 1933. In 1977 it was declared a Biosphere Reserve under the UNESCO Man and the Biosphere Programme. For these reasons it has attracted scientific interest. The Department of Parks, Wildlife and Heritage of the Tasmanian Government is responsible for the management of the Macquarie Island Nature Reserve.

57 **Biogeography and ecology in Tasmania.**
Edited by W. D. Williams.   The Hague: W. Junk Publishers, 1974.
498p. maps. bibliogs. (Monographiae Biologicae, vol. 25).

This is the first major biological study of Tasmania, which climatically and geologically differs markedly from mainland Australia. The sixteen chapters are written by experts in their respective fields and the text is consequently pitched at that level, although parts are intelligible to the informed layman. Detailed bibliographies follow each chapter.

Fauna

58 **Wildlife Tasmania.**
   Dave Watts. Kettering: Peregrine Press, 1994. 24p.
Consists mainly of beautiful colour photographs of animals and birds found within the 1.4 million hectares which make up Tasmania's World Heritage Wilderness.

59 **Tasmanian wild life: a popular account of the furred land mammals, snakes and introduced mammals of Tasmania.**
   Michael Sharland.   Melbourne: Melbourne University Press, 1962. 86p.
A popular reference to all the mammals and snakes of Tasmania based on the author's personal observations and long experience with various species of wildlife in the island state. Separated from the mainland by Bass Strait, most of Tasmania's animals have characteristics which distinguish them from related species elsewhere. Sharland pays special attention to the two marsupial predators found only in Tasmania – the so-called tiger (thylacine) and the Tasmanian devil. The tiger is now believed to be extinct.

60 **Fauna of Tasmania handbook.**
   Various authors.   Hobart: Fauna of Tasmania Committee, University of Tasmania, 1979 to date.
This series of booklets by various authors aims to collate the information available about Tasmanian animals and stimulate interest in their further study. Two further series are produced: Posters; and Identification Charts. Titles issued to date are: no. 1 *Tasmanian Odonata* by Piers Allbrook (1979); no. 2 *Tasmanian bird atlas* by David Thomas (1979); no. 3 *Tasmanian echinoderms* by Alan Dartnell (1980); no. 4 *Tasmanian caddis-flies* by Arturs Neboiss (1981); no. 5 *Tasmanian land and freshwater molluscs* by B. J. Smith and R. C. Kershaw (1981); no. 6 *Tasmanian amphibians* by A. A. Martin and M. J. Littlejohn (1982); no. 7 *Tasmanian freshwater fish* by Wayne Fulton (1990). All booklets are illustrated and contain distribution maps for each species as well as bibliographies.

61 **The fauna of Tasmania: mammals.**
   R. H. Green.   Launceston: Potoroo Publishing, 1994. Rev. ed. 56p.
First published in 1973 as *The mammals of Tasmania*, this edition is planned as the first of a series of publications dealing with the vertebrate fauna of Tasmania. Subsequent parts will cover birds, reptiles, frogs and freshwater fish. This book is a general text on Tasmanian mammals and includes various aspects of their evolution, relationships, reproduction, behaviour and present status. The content is based upon the author's personal observations during his 30 years as zoologist with the Queen Victoria Museum and Art Gallery in Launceston. Another two relevant titles are: Dave Watts's *Tasmanian mammals: a field guide*, Rev. ed. 1993, and *Tasmania's native mammals* by Phil Andrews, issued in 1981.

62 **Thylacine: the tragedy of the Tasmanian tiger.**
Eric R. Guiler. Melbourne: Melbourne University Press, 1985. 207p. bibliog.

Traces the history of the Tasmanian tiger – the thylacine – Australia's largest carnivorous marsupial, from fossils and early Aboriginal paintings through to the present. The author assumes that the tiger still exists, although most experts believe it to have become extinct in the 1930s.

63 **The Tasmanian devil.**
Eric Guiler. Hobart: St David's Park Publishing, 1992. 28p.

Illustrated with many black-and-white photographs this large-format book tells the story of a year in the life of the nocturnal marsupial carnivore – the Tasmanian devil. It does not cover the complicated aspects of the devil's physiology and biochemistry, these being outside the scope of a brief review. Unlike its close relative the Tasmanian tiger, which is extinct, the devil is abundant in Tasmania.

64 **The fauna of Tasmania: birds.**
R. H. Green. Launceston: Potoroo Publishing, 1995. 170p.

About 299 of approximately 325 species of birds presently listed for Tasmania are included, those not mentioned being mostly rare visitors or vagrants. For a full list of the birds found in Tasmania, see the author's 1993 revised, fifth edition of *Birds of Tasmania: an annotated checklist with illustrations*. The present book is also illustrated with 192 colour photographs and the notes on each species give information about evolution and relationship, identification, distribution, seasonal movement, habitat preference, degree of abundance, food behaviour and breeding.

65 **A guide to the birds of Tasmania.**
Michael Sharland. Illustrations by Jane Burrell. Hobart: Drinkwater Publishing, 1981. 172p.

The guide covers just on 290 species of which 108 are illustrated, including all the Tasmanian endemics.

66 **Birds in Bass Strait.**
Ken Simpson. Sydney: Reed for B.H.P., 1972. 112p. maps. bibliog.

A well-illustrated survey of the birds which live around and migrate to Bass Strait, the expanse of water which separates Tasmania from the mainland.

67 **A bibliography of ornithology in Tasmania 1950-1993.**
Gillian Lord. Hobart: The Author, 1994. 2nd ed. 54p.

'Up to 1950 Tasmanian ornithological literature is covered by Major Whittell in *The literature of Australian birds* published in 1954 by Paterson Brokenshaw. This list therefore covers articles written since then.'

68   **Fishes of Tasmania.**
      P. R. Last, E. O. G. Scott, F. H. Talbot.   Hobart: Tasmanian Fisheries
      Development Authority, 1983. 563p. bibliog.
A comprehensive guide to Tasmanian fish fauna. It deals with 459 species. Each
species is illustrated, its shape and colour briefly described, its maximum size and
distribution noted, and some general remarks on each species are provided.

69   **Origins of the Tasmanian trout: an account of the Salmon Ponds
      and the first introduction of salmon and trout to Tasmania in 1864.**
      Jean Walker.   Hobart: Inland Fisheries Commission, 1988. 47p.
An illustrated historical booklet about the introduction of salmon and trout into
Tasmanian waters, which led to the island's becoming one of the foremost sports
fisheries in the world.

70   **Salmon of the Antipodes: a history and review of trout, salmon and
      char and introduced coarse fish in Australasia.**
      John Clements.   Ballarat, Victoria: The Author, 1988. 391p. bibliog.
A detailed history of the subject with many historical illustrations. Although the area
covered takes in the whole of Australia and New Zealand, Tasmania features
prominently in the text since the climatic conditions of the island favour these species
of fish.

71   **Butterflies of Tasmania.**
      Illustrations Julie Virtue. Text Peter McQuillan. Edited by Phil Collier.
      Hobart: Tasmanian Field Naturalists Club, 1994. 104p. bibliog.
This publication provides information to aid the identification of butterflies likely to
be encountered in Tasmania. All 39 known Tasmanian species are described and
illustrated with colour drawings.

72   **Catalogue of the insects of Tasmania.**
      T. D. Semmens, P. B. McQuillan, G. Hayhurst.   Hobart: Department of
      Primary Industry, 1992. 104p. bibliog.
The catalogue attempts, for the first time, to present an inventory of the described
insects which occur within the geopolitical boundaries of Tasmania, including the
major Bass Strait islands and the subantarctic Macquarie Island. Later editions will
include additional information for each entry such as reference to source, habitat,
preferences and endemism. An extensive 34-page bibliography of references to insects
of Tasmania is appended to the catalogue.

73   **Snails and slugs introduced to or pests in Tasmania.**
      Ron C. Kershaw.   Launceston: Queen Victoria Museum and Art
      Gallery, 1991. 67p. bibliog.
Provides descriptions and illustrations of slugs and snails found in Tasmania, both
introduced and native, which are pests.

74 **Tasmanian sea shells.**
  Margaret Richmond.   Devonport: The Author, 1990-91. 2 vols. maps.
  bibliogs.

An illustrated guide in colour to the most common shells found on Tasmanian beaches. Each shell is described and accompanied by a distribution map.

Flora

75 ´ **Guide to flowers and plants in Tasmania.**
  Launceston Field Naturalists Club. Edited by Mary Cameron.   Sydney:
  Reed, 1981. 120p. bibliog.

A non-technical book for the identification of wildflowers in Tasmania. Each colour photograph of a specimen is accompanied by a description of the plant. Not all 2000 species of flowering plants in Tasmania are featured – only a representative sample of those commonly seen have been chosen for inclusion in the book.

76 **The student's flora of Tasmania.**
  Winifred M. Curtis.   Hobart: St David's Park Publishing, 1993-94.
  5 vols.

Parts 1–4A were previously published from 1963 to 1979. With the completion of Part 4B, all five volumes were reissued, thus bringing to a successful conclusion a major project which spans the years 1948 to 1991.

77 **The endemic flora of Tasmania.**
  Winifred M. Curtis. Painted by Margaret Stones.   London: Ariel Press,
  1967-78. 6 vols. maps.

A major work on the island state's endemic plants, sponsored by Lord Talbot de Malahide, an avid collector and gardener who cultivated Tasmanian plants on his estate in Ireland. Margaret Stones, an Australian botanical artist employed at Kew, painted the specimens sent from Tasmania, and Winifred Curtis, the noted botanist, provided the text, which is short, scientifically accurate yet intelligible to the layman.

78 **Tasmania's rainforests.**
  Compiled by Bob Blakers, Robin Tindale, Ian Skinner.   Hobart: The
  Wilderness Society, 1986. 55p.

Consists mainly of beautiful colour photographs with a concise general introduction and shorter prefaces to rainforest regions. It should be used in conjuction with the next item *The rainforest of Tasmania* (q.v.).

79 **The rainforest of Tasmania.**
Working Group for Rainforest Conservation. Text by Peter Boyer, John
Hickey. Hobart: Tasmanian Government, 1987. 128p. bibliog.
The book was produced by an editorial team representing the Working Group for
Rainforest Conservation, which was established by the Tasmanian Government. The
book examines Tasmanian rainforest, which covers about 10 per cent of the island,
from many perpectives. Its purpose is both to provide general information about
rainforest and to point out the many values and uses which need to be considered
when making management decisions. It is intended primarily for the general public,
and the text which is easily comprehensible is aided by a multitude of colour
photographs. A much more technical book was published by the National Parks &
Wildlife Service in 1984 – *Rainforest in Tasmania*, by S. J. Jarman, M. J. Brown and
G. Kantvilas.

80 **Rainforest plants of Tasmania.**
Phil Collier. Hobart: Society for Growing Australian Plants,
Tasmanian Region, 1992. 65p. bibliog.
This booklet in the Plant Identikit series is a guide to the common species of rainforest
plants. Each species listed is accompanied by a colour illustration and descriptive
notes. Other booklets in the Identikit series, all by Phil Collier, are *Wildflowers of Mt
Wellington*, *Alpine wildflowers of Tasmania*, and *Woodland wildflowers of Tasmania*.

81 **Native trees of Tasmania.**
Text J. B. Kirkpatrick. Illustrations Sue Backhouse. Hobart: Sue
Backhouse, 1985. 135p. maps.
A listing of all trees native to Tasmania. There are illustrations of the leaves and
woody fruits of every tree, accompanied by a brief description and a distribution map.

82 **Orchids of Tasmania.**
Phil Collier. Hobart: Society for Growing Australian Plants,
Tasmanian Region, 1993. 97p. bibliog.
This booklet is a guide to the common orchids in Tasmania. About 100 species of
orchids out of about 180 in existence in Tasmania are illustrated and described.

83 **Historic Tasmanian gardens.**
Phyl Frazer Simons. Canberra: Mulini Press, 1987. 295p. bibliog.
A well-researched volume on Tasmania's historic gardens. A highlight of the book is
the large number of sketches, drawings and photographs.

84 **The Royal Tasmanian Botanical Gardens 1818-1986: a history in
stone, soil and superintendents.**
Marcus Hurburgh. Hobart: Shearwater Press, 1986. 8p. maps. bibliog.
A well-researched history of the gardens with many illustrations.

85   Van Diemen's Land correspondents: letters from R. C. Gunn,
      R. W. Lawrence, Jorgen Jorgenson, Sir John Franklin and others
      to Sir William J. Hooker 1827-1849.
      T. E. Burns, J. R. Skemp.   Launceston: Queen Victoria Museum, 1961.
      142p. map. (The Records of the Queen Victoria Museum, New Series,
      no. 14).
This collection of the letters between William Jackson Hooker, the English botanist,
and his botanical correspondents in Tasmania, chief of whom was the naturalist
Ronald Campbell Gunn, is not only of botanical interest but also a valuable
contribution to the early history of Tasmania. Joseph D. Hooker used the reports made
to his father from Gunn and others in a compilation of his monumental 4-volume work
on the flora of Tasmania, *Flora Tasmaniae*, published in London in 1860. A well-
researched, fictional account of Gunn by Nancy Cato, *A distant island*, was published
in 1988.

86   Aspects of Tasmanian botany: a tribute to Winifred Curtis.
      Edited by M. R. Banks and others.   Hobart: Royal Society for
      Tasmania, 1991. 247p. maps. bibliogs.
A collection of botanical papers written by specialists for specialists, published as a
tribute to the work of Dr Winifred Curtis who emigrated from England to Tasmania in
1939. Here she taught, wrote and lectured, and became involved in two major projects
on the botany of Tasmania, which resulted in *The student's flora of Tasmania*, 5 vols
(1993); and *The endemic flora of Tasmania*, 6 vols (1967-78) (q.v.).

History

General

87   A short history of Tasmania.
Lloyd Robson.   Melbourne: Oxford University Press, 1985. 189p.
A readable, concise yet comprehensive general history of Tasmania for the layman.
Those readers who are interested in a more detailed exposition of the themes raised in
this book are referred to the author's main work in two volumes: *A history of
Tasmania* (see item no. 88), published in 1983 and 1991 respectively. This *Short
History* is recommended as background reading for the tourist intending to visit
Tasmania.

88   A history of Tasmania.
Lloyd Robson.   Melbourne: Oxford University Press, 1983-91. 2 vols.
bibliog.
Volume 1 is subtitled *Van Diemen's Land from the earliest·times to 1855*. It has won
two important Australian book awards for the excellence of the writing. Volume 2,
Colony and state from 1856 to the 1980s, completes the story. Professor Robson was
ill with cancer when completing the second volume and died before its publication.

89   Tasmania: from colony to statehood 1803-1945.
W. A. Townsley.   Hobart: St David's Park Publishing, 1991. 477p.
bibliog.
As a political scientist, the author tells this history of Tasmania in terms of the growth
and shaping of legal and political institutions.

90 **Tasmania: microcosm of the federation or a vassal state, 1945-1983.**
W. A. Townsley. Hobart: St David's Park Publishing, 1994. 451p.
bibliog.

The author's continuation of the history of Tasmania from the first volume *Tasmania: from colony to statehood 1803-1945*, published in 1991 (see item no. 89).

91 **The golden years of Tasmania: from boom to almost bust and back again in the island state, Tasmania.**
David L. Hopkins. Hobart: St David's Park Publishing, 1991. 271p.

A history of Tasmania in black-and-white contemporary photographs. The emphasis is on economic developments such as agriculture and mining. The pictures (unintentionally) provide harsh evidence of how unfettered development leads to environmental degradation.

92 **Historic Tasmania sketchbook.**
Drawings by Max Angus, Frank Mather, Arthur Phillips. Text by Patsy Adam-Smith, Joan Woodberry. Adelaide: Rigby, 1977. 250p.

An omnibus volume containing *Nineteenth century Tasmania, Hobart, Launceston, Port Arthur*, all published previously in Rigby's Sketchbook Series. The book tells the stories of many of Tasmania's oldest buildings. All are illustrated with drawings by some of Australia's best-known artists.

93 **The history of Tasmania.**
John West. Edited by A. G. L. Shaw. Sydney: Angus & Robertson, in association with the Royal Australian Historical Society, 1971. 699p.
bibliog.

First published in 1852, this is still a perceptive and useful history of early Tasmania by an intelligent, contemporary observer. West was a journalist, Congregational minister and anti-transportation leader who had arrived in Van Diemen's Land in 1838. Professor Shaw has prepared this edition in the form which West had proposed for his planned second edition in 1853, and has annotated the text for the modern reader. An extensive bibliography, including works published after 1851, is appended.

94 **A history of Tasmania from its discovery in 1642 to the present time.**
James Fenton. Hobart: Melanie Publications, 1984. 462p. map.
bibliog.

This facsimile edition of a general history of Tasmania, first published in 1884, is still a useful source of information especially for the neglected period from the 1840s until the 1880s. Fenton is sympathetic to the Aborigines and the book contains reproductions of four portraits of Aborigines by the colonial portraitist Thomas Bock.

95 **Early Tasmania: papers read before the Royal Society of Tasmania during the years 1888-1899.**
James Backhouse Walker. Hobart: Government Printer, 1950. 294p. maps.

Walker, solicitor and historian and active in public affairs, was a regular contributor to the proceedings of the Royal Society of Tasmania. Most of his papers on the discovery, early settlement and Aboriginal inhabitants of Tasmania were published posthumously in 1902. Reprinted several times since, the book remained a standard work for many years, until superseded as a result of the discovery of source material that was not accessible to Walker.

96 **Tasmanian insights: essays in honour of Geoffrey Thomas Stilwell.**
Edited by Gillian Winter. Hobart: State Library of Tasmania, 1992. 245p. bibliogs.

This publication stems from a wide community recognition of the contribution made by G. T. Stilwell, Curator of the Allport Library and Museum of Fine Arts, State Library of Tasmania, towards research and study into many aspects of Tasmanian history. The book contains a collection of essays by specialists on historical topics which have been of interest to Stilwell. They are a lasting addition to Tasmanian historical studies.

97 **The flow of culture: Tasmanian studies.**
Edited by Michael Roe. Canberra: Australian Academy of the Humanities, 1987. 146p.

The papers which make up this book were presented at a meeting of the Australian Academy of the Humanities, held in Hobart on 11-13 July 1986. The academic contributors consider European and especially British influences on the new frontier-colonial society. The culture of the indigenous people – the Aborigines – is also considered.

Foundation

98 **Account of a voyage to establish a settlement in Bass's Straits, to which is added a description of Port Philip and an account of the landing at the Derwent in 1804.**
Edited from the despatches of David Collins Esq. Lieut.-Governor, by John Currey. Melbourne: Colony Press, 1986. 258p. map. bibliog.

This volume, based on despatches held in the British Colonial Office in London, is a rare eyewitness report on the aborted settlement of Port Phillip in Victoria and Risdon Cove on the Derwent, and an excellent account of the first year in the life of Sullivan's Cove – the first permanent settlement in Van Diemen's Land. There is a lengthy introduction and explanatory notes to Collins's text by the editor. The book is a 'foundation document'. A second-hand account of Collins's association with Van

Diemen's Land can be found in C. R. Collins's *Saga of settlement: a brief account of the life and times of Lieutenant-Colonel David Collins 1st Judge Advocate of the Colony of New South Wales and Lieutenant-Governor of Southern Van Diemen's Land*, published in 1956.

99 **Convicts unbound: the story of the 'Calcutta' convicts and their settlement in Australia.**
Marjorie Tipping. Melbourne: Viking O'Neil, 1988. 353p. bibliog.
A detailed, scholarly study of the 307 convicts who left England on H.M.S. *Calcutta* to found the colony of Port Phillip (Victoria) in 1803, failed and seven months later sailed to Tasmania, where they established the colony of Hobart Town, the second settlement in Van Diemen's Land. The author traces the descendants of the convicts, many of whom became prominent citizens in both Tasmania and Victoria.

Colonial period

100 **Land settlement in early Tasmania: creating an antipodean England.**
Sharon Morgan. Cambridge: Cambridge University Press, 1992. 214p. maps. bibliog.
Based on primary sources this is the only detailed, scholarly investigation of land alienation and land use by white settlers in Tasmania. It treats the first decades of settlement and deals with the effects of the European invasion on Aboriginal society, the early history of environmental degradation, the island's social history and the growth of primary industry. The book offers a valuable international perspective, presenting Van Diemen's Land as a case-study of nineteenth-century European expansion and imperialism.

101 **The struggle for self-government in Tasmania 1842-1856.**
W. A. Townsley. Hobart: L. G. O'Shea, Government Printer, 1951. 174p.
A study of the constitutional conflicts in Tasmania which eventually led to the establishment of the colony's first fully representative two-chamber parliament. At the time of writing the author was senior lecturer in history and political science at the University of Tasmania.

102 **A geographical, historical, and topographical description of Van Diemen's Land, with important hints to emigrants . . .**
George William Evans. Melbourne: Heinemann, 1967. 140p. map.
This book was first published in 1822 by Evans, Surveyor General of Van Diemen's Land and explorer of the mainland, with the purpose of expanding the numbers of free settlers from England. It can be regarded as an early, celebratory guide book to Tasmania. The separate chart included in the book and compiled from Evans's own

surveys was unique as it was the first to be published which showed the areas of land granted to the settlers in Van Diemen's Land. This facsimile edition of Evans's 1822 text also contains an introductory note giving publishing details of the book and biographical details of Evans by Karl R. Von Stieglitz. A full-length biography of Evans was published by A. K. Weatherburn in 1966, entitled *George William Evans: explorer.*

103   **A picture of Van Diemen's Land.**
David Burn.   Hobart: Cat & Fiddle Press, 1973. 185p.
First published in serial form in the *Colonial Magazine* of 1840-41. Although anecdotal in parts, this facsimile reprint provides general background history of Van Diemen's Land to the late 1830s from the point of view of a contemporary observer.

104   **The history of Van Diemen's Land from the year 1824 to 1835, inclusive: during the Administration of Lieutenant-Governor George Arthur.**
Henry Melville. Edited with an introduction, notes and commentary by George Mackaness.   Sydney: Horwitz-Grahame, 1965. 199p.
When Melville's book originally appeared in 1835, it was a pioneering work because it indicated the evils of the convict transportation system and also the colonial autocracy of Governor Arthur. In disregard of the prevalent sentiments he viewed the Aborigines with sympathy. Concluding the book he advocated progressive change towards expanding the power of the free settlers. Due to its original theme, the *History* is a contemporary document of great importance.

105   **Andrew Bent and the freedom of the press in Van Diemen's Land.**
Joan Woodberry.   Hobart: Fullers Bookshop, 1972. 174p. bibliog.
A study of the controversy about freedom of the press in Van Diemen's Land between 1823 and 1929 during Sir George Arthur's governorship of the colony. It is also the story of Andrew Bent, a convict printer, who, after receiving a pardon, owned the *Hobart Town Gazette*, which was in the forefront of the battle for press freedom.

106   **The early history of Tasmania. Volume II: The penal settlement era, 1804-18, Collins, Sorell and Arthur.**
R. W. Giblin. Edited with additions from the author's notes by J. D. A. Collier.   Melbourne: Melbourne University Press, in association with Oxford University Press, 1939. 709p. bibliog.
This is a continuation of Giblin's *The early history of Tasmania: the geographical era 1642-1804* published in 1928 (q.v.). It is a very detailed study of early settlement up to 1826 when the text ends abruptly because of the author's death. The work was edited for publication by J. D. A. Collier of the Tasmanian Public Library.

107 **Sir George Arthur, Bart. 1784-1854: Superintendent of British Honduras, Lieutenant-Governor of Van Diemen's Land and of Upper Canada, Governor of Bombay Presidency.**
A. G. L. Shaw.   Melbourne: Melbourne University Press, 1980. 307p. bibliog.

Unusually for this period of the British Empire, when colonial administrators enjoyed short tenures, Arthur held four consecutive, top administrative posts in various colonies. The eminent historian Professor Shaw devotes a substantial part of the book to the Tasmanian years and brings to life not only Arthur, but also life in the colony of Van Diemen's Land at the time. This biography compares more than favourably with M. C. I. Levy's earlier biography *Governor George Arthur: a colonial benevolent despot*, published in 1953.

108 **Sir John Franklin in Tasmania 1837-1843.**
Kathleen Fitzpatrick.   Melbourne: Melbourne University Press, 1949. 408p. bibliog.

Sir John Franklin, R.N., the polar explorer, was the fifth Governor of Tasmania. This book, mainly based on research in manuscript sources, examines Franklin's administrative record in Tasmania during his controversial six years in office.

109 **Varieties of vice-regal life.**
Sir William Denison.   London: Longmans Green, 1870. 2 vols.

Sir William Thomas Denison was Lieutenant-General of Van Diemen's Land from early 1847 to early 1855, when he was appointed Governor of New South Wales and (nominally) Governor-General of the Australian colonies, He left New South Wales in 1861 to become Governor of Madras. More than half of the first volume of the autobiography, some 230 pages, consists of his journal and extracts from letters while he was in Tasmania. It gives a picture of the administration of the colony and the conditions prevailing in Tasmania then, as it were, 'from the horse's mouth'.

110 **Mortmain: Van Diemen's Land.**
Collected and transcribed by Eustace Fitzsymonds.   Hobart: Sullivan's Cove, Publisher, 1977. 262p.

In this volume appear reprints of petitions and requests sent to Governors Sorell, Arthur, Franklin, Eardley-Wilmot and Denison or to high government officials, by convicts and free settlers, native-born and new arrivals, deserted husbands and wronged wives, notables and nonentities. The earliest is dated 1819, the latest 1854. Appended to the ingratiating petitions are the terse observations of Governors and officials on the merits of the application. It makes for great reading for the layman and furnishes rich material for the historian. Fitzsymonds repeated the exercise in 1980 with *A looking glass for Tasmania: letters, petitions and other manuscripts relating to Van Diemen's Land 1808-1845*. Appearing in chronological order, they range from 1808 to 1845, but the majority are from 1824 to 1836, the period of George Arthur, who, more than any other Governor, interested himself in the minutiae of colonial administration.

111   **The diaries and letters of G. T. W. B. Boyes. Volume 1 1820-1832.**
Edited by Peter Chapman.   Melbourne: Oxford University Press,
1985. 692p. bibliog.
Boyes was a senior public servant in Van Diemen's Land from 1826 until his death in
1853. This is the first volume of his diaries and letters which together comprise some
600,000 words. A second volume will cover the period 1832 to 1842 and a third the
years 1842 to 1853. Boyes was a cultivated man – 24 of his sketches and watercolours
are reproduced in this book – well read and musical. His standing in Hobart society
makes for a compelling account of the colonial experience, the whole being well
supported by a scholarly editorial apparatus, including an informed bibliographical
introduction, excellent footnotes, an exhaustive bibliography and a detailed index.

112   **Journals of the Land Commissioners for Van Diemen's Land
1826-28.**
Edited by Anne McKay, with an introduction by P. R. Eldershaw.
Hobart: University of Tasmania, in conjunction with the Tasmanian
Historical Research Association, 1962. 151p. maps. bibliog.
The Land Commissioners were appointed by Lieutenant-Governor George Arthur to
examine properties in the settled districts of Van Diemen's Land for valuation
purposes. As part of the official report to Arthur, the *Journals* are of value to the
historian since they reveal the extent of settlement at the time. They also provide
comment on pastoral practices, the land system, Aborigines and bushrangers.

113   **Land musters, stock returns and lists: Van Diemen's Land
1803-1822.**
Edited by Irene Schaffer.   Hobart: St David's Park Publishing, 1991.
254p. bibliog.
From the foundation of European settlement, musters were utilized by the colonial
authorities to keep records of the officials, military, free settlers and convicts and their
families, and later to record their land and stock holdings. This compilation of the
musters for the first 20 years of settlement gives a unique insight, as well as raw
material for researchers, of the growth of the young colony in great detail.

114   **Historical records of Australia.**
Melbourne: Library Committee of the Commonwealth Parliament,
1914-25. 33 vols.
This major series of Australia's historical documents contains mainly despatches and
enclosures of the early Governors to the authorities in England. Series 3, consisting of
6 volumes entitled *Despatches and papers relating to the settlement of the States*,
provides invaluable primary source material for the early history of Tasmania.

Hobart

115 **Hobart Town.**
Peter Bolger.   Canberra: Australian National University Press, 1973.
237p. bibliog.
A social history of the growth of the city of Hobart from its earliest days as a convict
settlement to a metropolis of the late nineteenth century. The author is an academic
historian and a graduate of the University of Tasmania.

116 **Urbanization: the evolution of an Australian capital.**
R. J. Solomon.   Sydney: Angus & Robertson, 1976. 434p. maps.
bibliog.
This scholarly book analyses in great detail the development of Hobart, the capital of
Tasmania, from its establishment as Australia's second settlement in 1803 to the city
of the 1960s.

117 **Hobart.**
Lloyd Robson, Gordon Rimmer.   In: *The origins of Australia's
capital cities.*   Edited by Pamela Statham.   Cambridge: Cambridge
University Press, 1990, p. 77-117.
Lloyd Robson's chapter *Settling Van Diemen's Land* and Gordon Rimmer's *Hobart: a
moment of glory* answer the twin questions: why Hobart was situated where it now
stands, and how it was established.

118 **Old Hobart Town and environs 1802-1855.**
Carolyn R. Stone, Pamela Tyson.   Melbourne: Pioneer Design Studio,
1978. 208p. maps. bibliog.
A presentation in contemporary pictures and words of what Hobart was like during the
years 1802 to 1855. The book contains 129 reproductions of sketches, lithographs,
etchings, aquatints, watercolours and oil paintings by famous contemporary artists.
Documentary material includes extracts from letters, diaries and records of
Tasmania's first eight Governors. This large-format book was voted Book of the Year
for Tasmanian-oriented publications.

119 **This southern outpost: Hobart 1846-1914.**
Julia Clark.   Hobart: Corporation of the City of Hobart, 1988. 88p.
bibliog.
The book is based on an exhibition of photographs mounted in Hobart for the
Australian Bicentennial in 1988. The arrangement of the photographs and the linking
text succeeds admirably in presenting nearly seventy years of Hobart's history.

120 **Old Hobart Town today: a photographic essay.**
Frank Bolt.   Hobart: Waratah Publications, 1981. 256p. bibliog.
This is a professional photographer's pictorial record of historic Hobart, Australia's
second-oldest city. The black-and-white photographs are accompanied by extensive
historical captions.

121 **Victorian and Edwardian Hobart from old photographs.**
Introduction and commentaries by Dan Sprod.   Sydney: John
Ferguson, 1977. unpaged.
Contains 204 photographs from the beginnings of photography in Tasmania in the late
1840s to 1910 when King Edward VII died. It is an interesting pictorial record of the
built and natural environment of Tasmania's capital as well as of the diverse activities
of the inhabitants of the city.

122 **'Down Wapping': Hobart's vanished Wapping and Old Wharf
districts.**
The Wapping History Group.   Hobart: Blubber Head Press, 1988.
251p. maps. bibliog.
This book was initiated when the seven contributors were postgraduate students in the
history department of the University of Tasmania. They have written a lively history
of a commercial and residential dockside area of Hobart which began to decline
during World War I. Many interesting illustrations add to the text. The book was
reprinted with corrections and a new map in 1994.

123 **The West Hobart story.**
Joan Goodrick.   Hobart: Shearwater Press, 1993. 217p. maps. bibliog.
A chatty non-focused account of the development of an old inner-city suburb. An
ideal companion to take on a stroll around the area, as every street is chronicled. There
are many black-and-white photographs of streetscapes and buildings.

124 **Glenorchy 1804-1964.**
Alison Alexander. Sketches and maps by Mollie Tomlin.   Hobart:
Glenorchy City Council, 1986. 382p. bibliog.
An excellent account of the Hobart municipality of Glenorchy by a professional
historian. The book is based on documentary sources, some 200 oral interviews with
residents and is enhanced by more than 350 photographs.

125 **Taroona 1808-1986: farm lands to a garden suburb.**
Written by past and present residents of Taroona.   Hobart: Taroona
Historical Group, 1988. 360p. maps.
The book has 108 contributors who have written 113 articles and gathered together
235 photographs and maps of Taroona, a southern suburb of Hobart. Understandably
the quality of the writing and research varies widely. However, this large volume is
the first and only record of the area, and it is noteworthy because it has been written
by the people who live in the community.

Regional and local history

126 The valley of the Derwent.
L. S. Bethell.   Hobart: L. G. Shea, Government Printer, 1960. 139p.
maps. bibliogs.

Covers much of the history of southern Tasmania up to 1850 and provides a
companion volume to the author's earlier book *The story of Port Dalrymple: life and
work in northern Tasmania*, published in 1957 and reissued in 1980 (q.v.).

127 The romance of the Huon River.
A. H. Garnsey.   Melbourne: Whitcombe & Tombs, 1947. 219p. map.

An anecdotal, romanticized history of the Huon River Valley, south of Hobart, with
no bibliography or index. It is nevertheless a useful general introduction to the region.

128 The story of Port Dalrymple: life and work in northern Tasmania.
Llewelyn Slingsby Bethell.   Hobart: Blubber Head Press, 1980. 193p.
maps.

A facsimile edition of the book first published in 1957. It is a history of northern
Tasmania, including the city of Launceston, for the first hundred years of its white
settlement, i.e. up to the date of Federation. Many black-and-white illustrations
accompany the text.

129 George Town: history of the town and district.
J. G. Branagan.   Launceston: Regal Publications, 1994. 183p. bibliog.

Illustrated with many original photographs, this is a popular history of the George
Town district situated on Port Dalrymple on the River Tamar estuary. It is written by a
local resident of many years, a retired farmer who is not a trained historian.

130 Pioneers of Burnie: a sesquicentenary publication 1827-1977.
Richard Pike.   Burnie: R. Pike, 1977. 100p.

A history of Burnie told through the lives of early settlers who came to Burnie in the
19th century and who have descendants living in the municipality.

131 Of rascals and rusty relics: an introduction to north east Tasmania.
G. Miller, S. Miller.   Hobart: OBM, 1979. 106p. map. bibliog.

An introductory history of the north-east of Tasmania with many black-and-white
photographs.

132 The historic Tamar valley: its people, places and shipping 1798-1990.
J. G. Branagan.   Launceston: Real Publications, 1994. 316p. maps.
bibliog.

A chronological compilation of people, places and events which played a part in the
development of the Tamar Valley in north-east Tasmania, written by an enthusiastic
amateur historian. There are a large number of illustrations.

133 **With the pioneers.**
Charles Ramsay.   Hobart: National Trust of Australia (Tasmania),
La Trobe Group, 1979. 2nd rev. ed. 305p. maps. bibliog.
Originally published in 1957, the second edition of this book revises and corrects the
original text and index and adds a bibliography. It traces the history of the white
settlement and the development of the Devonport region in north-west Tasmania. The
period covered is from 1798 to the end of the 19th century.

134 **The story of Devonport.**
C. J. Binks.   Devonport: City Council, 1981. 57p. bibliog.
This outline of the story of Devonport's growth from its establishment to the present
has been written to mark the occasion of the conferring of city status upon Devonport
on 21 April 1981.

135 **As the river flows.**
Co-authors and compilers: Dorothy Beswick, Alec Edwards, Helen
Stingel, Elsie Targett, Charles Taylor. Edited by Geoff Willson.
Ringarooma: Ringarooma Council, with the aid of the Australian
Bicentennial Authority, 1988. 231p.
A communal effort to present 'some of the history and stories of the Ringarooma
Municipality', situated in the north-eastern corner of Tasmania. Written by many
hands, the book is of uneven standard, and sources are not acknowledged. Many
black-and-white photographs are included.

136 **And wealth for toil: a history of northwest and western Tasmania
1825-1900.**
Kerry Pink.   Burnie: Advocate Marketing Services for Harris and
Company, 1990. 387p. maps. bibliog.
A comprehensive history of the exploration and settlement of the north-west and west
coast regions of Tasmania. The flavour of the text can be gleaned from the journalist
author's statement in the preface: 'The book is a tribute to the pioneering men and
women who transformed a primeval wilderness to an area we of the present generation
believe to be unsurpassed in Australia.' There are a multitude of historical illustrations,
mainly photographic, which mingle with contemporary colour photographs of the built
and natural landscape of the region.

137 **Around Circular Head.**
Pauline Yvette Buckley.   Launceston: Denbar Publishers, 1984. 141p.
bibliog.
A local history of the area around Stanley in north-west Tasmania. Over half of the
book tells the story of Trefoil Island, a tiny place off Cape Grim which, among other
things, supported a thriving muttonbirding industry. Many interesting photographs
support the text.

138 **Beyond the ramparts: a bicentennial history of Circular Head.**
Kerry Pink, Annette Ebdon. Smithton: Circular Head Bicentennial
History Group, 1988. 268p. maps.
A popular history, based on primary sources and anecdotal material, of the north-
western corner of Tasmania, including the off-shore islands. The book is well
illustrated.

139 **Waratah – pioneer of the west.**
Margery Godfrey. Waratah: Municipality of Waratah, 1984. 119p.
map. bibliog.
Mining and the timber trade have been the 'raison d'être' for Waratah municipality in
the north-west of Tasmania. The book, based mainly on anecdotal accounts as well as
written sources, records community life and experience against the background of
district mining, which followed the discovery of the rich Mt Bischoff lode in 1871.
This was not only the first major Tasmanian mine but also a major mine by world
standards. Many contemporary photographs accompany the text.

140 **Pioneers of Tasmania's west coast.**
C. J. Binks. Hobart: Blubber Head Press, 1988. 190p. maps.
Binks describes the origin and development of the isolated community on the west
coast of Tasmania. The text is informed by the 19th-century idea of progress.
Economically mainly dependent on the mining industry, the population has always
been vulnerable and resistance to change is deeply ingrained in the communities. This
conservatism may in large part explain the intensity and bitterness of the struggle to
save the south-west wilderness area in the 1970s and early 1980s. Many illustrations
accompany the text.

141 **Through Hell's Gates: a history of Strahan and Macquarie
Harbour.**
Kerry Pink. Burnie: The Advocate Newspaper, 1984. 90p.
Written for the general reader and tourist to the area by a long-time journalist with the
Advocate newspaper in Burnie, the book tells the story of Macquarie Harbour and the
Gordon River from their discovery in 1815 to the national controversy surrounding
the proposed Lower Gordon hydro-electric dam and the conservationist blockade of
1982-83.

142 **The wild west of Tasmania: being a description of the silver fields
of Zeehan and Dundas.**
Wilberton Tilley. Zeehan: Evershed Bros, 1891. 93 + xxv p.
An enthusiastic portrayal of the 'wild west coast' in the latter years of last century, the
book also includes the history of the region, much tabulation and description of the
mines of the day as well as a depiction of community life.

143   **Western Tasmania: a land of riches and beauty.**
Charles Whitham.   Queenstown: Board of Management, Robert Sticht
Memorial Library, 1949. 2nd ed. 158p. maps. bibliog.

The first edition of this well-regarded guide book to western Tasmania was published
in 1924. It contains much information on history and mining. The 1949 edition
includes a 'Brief description of mines and works at Mount Lyell Tasmania', described
as 'authorised' by the company's general manager.

144   **A terrible beauty: history of the Gordon River country.**
Richard Flanagan.   Melbourne: Greenhouse, 1985. 100p. bibliog.

Flanagan, a Rhodes scholar, is well qualified to write about Tasmania's south-west
wilderness. He spent his childhood there and since then has travelled the wild rivers of
the region by canoe. The Franklin river, made famous during the anti-dam battles in
the late 1970s and early 1980s, he has traversed thirteen times.

145   **Trampled wilderness: the history of southwest Tasmania.**
Ralph and Kathleen Gowlland.   Devonport: C. L. Richmond, 1977.
2nd ed. 205p. maps.

A history of south-west Tasmania based on diaries, memoirs and reminiscences of the
original pioneers. Many maps illustrate routes taken by the original explorers of the
region and there are many photographs and other illustrations.

146   **The roof of Tasmania: a history of the Central Plateau.**
Tim Jetson.   Launceston: Pelion Press, 1989. 174p. maps. bibliog.

A detailed history of the Central Plateau, a sparsely populated region of rugged
beauty, which attracted attention because of its reserves of natural resources. Fishing,
trapping, timber and water power as well as wool production were readily available
for exploitation by the colonists and their descendants. The underlying objective of the
author, an academic at the University of Tasmania, is to trace the interaction between
man and the environment in the region.

147   **Bothwell: the gateway to the Highlands.**
Gwen Webb.   Launceston: Regal Publications, 1990. 204p.

An amateur local history of Bothwell and the Central Tasmanian Lakes. A similar
booklet on the town was published by J. S. Weeding in 1988, entitled *A history of
Bothwell Tasmania*. Both books lack indexes and neither acknowledges sources.

148   **Campbell Town Tasmania: history and centenary of municipal
government.**
Historical Committee of the National Trust of Australia (Tasmania).
Campbell Town: Campbell Town Municipal Council, 1966. 356p.
maps.

A comprehensive history of Campbell Town, a small pastoral and agricultural town in
eastern Tasmania situated on the main road between Hobart and Launceston. It
concentrates on the early and mid 19th century. No acknowledgement of sources is
made.

149   **A history of the Lower Midlands.**
      J. S. Weeding.   Hobart: Cat & Fiddle Press, 1975. 135p.

Written by a long-time resident of the district and enthusiastic local historian, this is a factual as well as anecdotal account of the Lower Midlands, the gateway to the Central Highlands in the eastern part of Tasmania, centred on the township of Oatlands. Weeding published *A history of Oatlands* in 1988, a similar popular history with emphasis on the township and how prominent individuals influenced community life. Interesting period photographs are included in both books.

150   **The East Coasters: the early pioneering history of the east coast of Tasmania.**
      Lois Nyman.   Launceston: Regal Publications, 1990. 236p. maps. bibliog.

The story of the first wave of settlers who arrived on Tasmania's east coast between 1821 and 1831.

151   **Spring Bay Tasmania: a social history.**
      Suzanne Lester.   Hobart: Artemis Publishing and Marketing Consultants, 1994. 244p.

A thematic history of the Spring Bay region on the east coast centred around the towns of Orford and Triabunna. A wide range of sources have been used, including information derived from interviews. There is also a good selection of photographs. The thematic approach has created some unnecessary duplication in the text.

152   **'Thanks to providence': a history of Falmouth, Tasmania and its people.**
      Tim McManus.   Falmouth: The Author, 1993. 390p. maps. bibliog.

A minutely documented history of Falmouth, a small settlement on the east coast of Tasmania. The author, a resident of the township for 30 years, bases his narrative on extensive research both in printed sources and many interviews, as well as personal observations. The text is supplemented with a comprehensive collection of period photographs.

153   **Dire Strait: a history of Bass Strait.**
      Charles Bateson.   Sydney: Reed for B.H.P., 1973. 112p. maps. bibliog.

A comprehensive history of Bass Strait, which separates Tasmania from the Australian mainland, and its many islands which mostly are part of Tasmania. There are numerous dramatic illustrations, many of them in colour.

154   **First visitors to Bass Strait.**
      J. S. Cumpston.   Canberra: Roebuck Society, 1973. 103p. maps. bibliog. (Roebuck Society Publication, no. 7).

Cumpston's work consists of two parts: Part I: *The Furneaux Group, Bass Strait: first visitors, 1779-1810*; Part II: *Oiling at King Island, 1800-1810*. The book is a valuable contribution to the early history of Bass Strait and its islands.

155 The legends of Hunter Island.
Pauline Buckby.   Hobart: Shift 85, 1990. 200p. maps.

An anecdotal history of Hunter Island, lying off the north-west tip of Tasmania in Bass Strait. *Robbins Island saga*, published two years earlier, deals in a similar fashion with a neighbouring island. The latter book won for the author the award for the Fellowship of Australian Writers for the best local history published in Australia in 1988 – the Bicentenary year.

156 Maria Island: a Tasmanian Eden.
Maggie Weidenhofer.   Melbourne: B. & M. Reid, in association with Port Arthur Historic Site Management Authority, 1991. 3rd ed. 64p. maps. bibliog.

Maria Island lies off the east coast of Tasmania. It covers an area of 9672 hectares and is separated by a sea passage of about 5 kilometres at its nearest point to the coast of Tasmania. After a colourful history, well told in this book, it is now a national park. There are many illustrations both in colour and in black-and-white.

157 South Bruny Island – Tasmania: a brief history of its settlement.
Compiled by Richard Cobden Pybus.   Hobart: R. C. and B. J. Pybus, 1988. 257p. maps.

This is more in the form of a chronicle than an interpretative history. Sadly there is no index and no consolidated bibliography although references to sources used are given at the end of each chapter. The contemporary photographs are interesting.

158 Macquarie Island.
J. S. Cumpston.   Melbourne: Antarctic Division, Department of External Affairs Australia, 1968. 380p. maps. bibliog. (ANARE Scientific Reports, Series A (1), Narrative: Publication no. 93).

The subantarctic Macquarie Island has been a dependency of the State of Tasmania since 1825, when Van Diemen's Land was separated from New South Wales and created a separate colony. The island is about 32 km long and 4 km wide and lies some 800 nautical miles south-east of Tasmania. This narrative covers the period from the discovery of Macquarie Island by an Australian sealer in 1810 until it was declared a Sanctuary for birds and animals in 1933. Through much of its history large-scale sealing and boiling down of penguins for their oil had led to public outcry against the practice. Seventy historical photographs depict human activities on the island.

Biographies and Autobiographies

159 **The jubilee history of Tasmania illustrated: with which is incorporated the Early history of Victoria, Biographical sketches, & Australian representative men.**
T. W. H. Leavitt.   Melbourne: Wells and Leavitt, 1888. 2 vols.

A general outline of Tasmania's history; today the work's main usefulness rests in the biographical information it provides.

160 **Notable Tasmanians.**
R. A. Ferrall.   Launceston: Foot & Playsted, 1980. 204p.

The author, after a long career in business and public affairs, recalls the many prominent personalities with whom he was associated in his lifetime. A further collection of profiles of people who have played leading roles in Tasmanian affairs was published by Ferrall in 1982. It was entitled *Tasmanians all*.

161 **Women to remember.**
Veda Veale.   St. Helens: The Author, 1981. 111p.

Biographies of thirteen Tasmanian women who have contributed to the island's history.

162 **Flotsam and jetsam: floating fragments of life in England and Tasmania, an autobiographical sketch. With an outline of the introduction of responsible government.**
Henry Button.   Launceston: Regal Press, 1993. 471p.

Button joined the *Launceston Examiner* newspaper in 1845 at the age of sixteen. The newspaper was to be his life's work for much of the nineteenth century. He became joint-owner of the paper in 1857 and sole proprietor in 1887. His autobiography is a fascinating record of Tasmania's social history. The present edition is a facsimile reprint of the original book published in 1909, with an additional comprehensive index compiled in the late 1960s.

163   **Bush life in Tasmania fifty years ago: an account of pioneer work in Devon ... etc.**
James Fenton.   Launceston: Regal Publications, 1989. Centenary ed. 203p. map.

This is a reprint of the book first published in 1891, which tells of the author's pioneering experiences in Devon Tasmania from the time he began farming near Port Sorell in 1838. Besides containing a wealth of historical information the author's agreeable style of writing makes this an entertaining book. Fenton has also written *A history of Tasmania from its discovery in 1642 to the present time* which was published in 1984 (see item no. 94).

164   **Bartley of 'Kerry Lodge': a portrait of a pioneer in Van Diemen's Land.**
Yvonne A. Phillips.   Blackwell: The Author, 1987. 144p. map. bibliog.

Theodore Bartley (1803-78) settled in Van Diemen's Land in 1819 on 500 acres of land near Launceston. Being educated and articulate, he had something to say on most issues of the day. More than half of the book consists of original letters, addresses and newspaper articles containing his opinions on diverse matters of public interest. The book is valuable for this contemporary opinon.

165   **Partly personal: recollections of a one-time Tasmanian journalist.**
R. A. Ferrall.   Hobart: Cat & Fiddle Press, 1974. 140p.

The author has long been prominent in business and public affairs in Launceston. In this book he remembers his own career as well as many people who played important roles in Tasmanian society and affairs. In 1995, at the age of 90, Ferrall published an autobiography entitled *90 years on: a Tasmanian story.*

166   **There was a ship: the story of her years at sea.**
Patsy Adam-Smith.   Melbourne: Penguin Books, 1995. 284p.

A very readable account of the author's experiences on wooden ships sailing and trading among the Tasmanian islands in Bass Strait in the 1950s. The text has been updated and rewritten from two of Adam-Smith's earlier books *Moonbird people* (1965) and *There was a ship* (1967). It is a nostalgic story of a way of life which has now passed.

167   **The way my father tells it: the story of an Australian life.**
Tim Bowden.   Sydney: Australian Broadcasting Corporation, 1990. 276p.

John Bowden, the father of journalist and author Tim Bowden, was born in Hobart in 1906 and apart from the war years has spent all his life in Tasmania. This book, adapted from tape recordings from father to son, is the life-story of an 'everyman' growing up and living in Tasmania. It offers much raw material for Tasmanian social history.

168 **Island affair.**
Eleanor Albiston.   Melbourne: Esplanade Books, 1989. 176p.

Continues the story begun in *Escape to an island*, first published in 1966 and now issued again in a uniform paperback edition with *Island affair*. It is the story of an English couple who left England after World War II and brought up a family on a farm on Three Hummock Island off the north-west coast of Tasmania in Bass Strait. Both books provide fascinating reading of pioneering life in harsh surroundings.

Convicts

169 **The convict settlers of Australia.**
   L. L. Robson.   Melbourne: Melbourne University Press, 1994. 2nd ed.
   229p. bibliog.
First published in 1965, this classic study, based on statistical sampling of early
convict records, examines systematically the origins and crimes of the convicts who
made up most of the population of Australia in its early years. A large part of the book
is devoted to the convicts who were transported to Tasmania.

170 **The fatal shore: a history of the transportation of convicts to
   Australia 1787-1868.**
   Robert Hughes.   London: Collins Harvill, 1987. 688p. maps. bibliog.
Hughes, an Australian, is art critic for *Time* magazine and the author of several well-
regarded books. In this big, well-written work he investigates the convict system in
Australia. In convict lore Tasmania, or Van Diemen's Land as it was known then,
always had the worst reputation for severity. Chapter 11 (p. 368-424) is devoted to the
Tasmanian experience and there are textual references to it throughout the volume.

171 **The convicts of Van Diemen's Land 1840-1853.**
   James F. H. Moore.   Hobart: Cat & Fiddle Press, 1976. 145p. bibliog.
An exhaustive computer analysis of records in the archives of the Library of Tasmania
relating to the convicts who were transported to Tasmania from 1840 to 1853, when
transportation ceased.

172 **Notorious strumpets and dangerous girls: convict women in Van
   Diemen's Land 1803-1829.**
   Phillip Tardif.   Sydney: Angus & Roberson, 1990. 1081p. bibliog.
A meticulous listing of the vital details about the convictions and colonial careers of
all the 1675 women sent to Van Diemen's Land as convicts during the colony's first

quarter-century. An introduction offers a concise but authoritative study of female convict transportation to Van Diemen's Land.

173 Governor Arthur's convict system, Van Diemen's Land, 1824-36: a study in colonization.

William Douglass Forsyth. London: Longmans, Green for the Royal Empire Society, 1935. 213p. bibliog. (Royal Empire Society. Imperial Studies, no. 10).

An early study, from the original records, of the penal system as it operated in Tasmania under Governor Arthur.

174 The convict probation system: Van Diemen's Land 1839-1854: a study of the probation system of convict discipline; together with C. J. Latrobe's 1847 report on its operation, and the 1845 report of James Boyd on the probation station at Darlington, Maria Island.

Commentary and notes by Ian Brand. Edited by M. N. Sprod. Hobart: Blubber Head Press, 1990. 284p. bibliog.

The probation system of convict discipline was peculiar to the colony of Van Diemen's Land where it was introduced, as an experiment, in 1839. Such was the experience of the system in the colony up to 1846, that it was thereafter greatly modified and gradually abandoned and never tried elsewhere.

175 Protest and punishment: the story of the social and political protesters transported to Australia 1788-1868.

George Rudé. Oxford: Clarendon Press, 1978. 270p. bibliog.

Contains a chapter on the protesters who were transported as convicts from England to Van Diemen's Land, and what became of them.

176 Ordered to the island: Irish convicts and Van Diemen's Land.

John Williams. Sydney: Crossing Press, 1994. 226p. bibliog.

Over 14,000 Irish convicts, both men and women, were transported to Tasmania between 1803 and 1853. The majority arrived during and after the Great Famine driven to their crimes by the extreme hunger and deprivation of that period. Detailed study of the individuals, their offences, trials, sentences and arrivals are linked by the author with official policies and prejudices to unravel the realities of transportation during the penal era.

177 To hell or to Hobart.

Patrick Howard. Sydney: Kangaroo Press, 1993. 199p. bibliog.

Irishman Patrick Howard traces his ancestor Stephen Howard's Irish roots, his trial and transportation to Van Diemen's Land, where, when pardoned, he married an Irish convict girl and became a farmer. Today, his descendants are still active in the mining industry. In telling the story of one Irish family, the author has managed to illustrate the whole Irish experience in convict Tasmania.

178   **William Smith O'Brien and his Irish revolutionary companions in penal exile.**
Blanche M. Towhill.   Columbia: University of Missouri Press, 1981.
269p. bibliog.

An historical account of seven Irishmen caught up in the Irish revolutionary struggle of 1848, convicted of either urging revolution or taking part in it and sent into penal exile as punishment for that involvement. The text deals primarily with their years of exile in the penal colony of Van Diemen's Land. The men were William Smith O'Brien, who was the recognized leader of the exiles, John Mitchel, Thomas Meagher, Patrick O'Donoghue, John Martin, Kevin O'Doherty and Terence McManus.

179   **The gardens of hell: John Mitchel in Van Diemen's Land 1850-1853.**
John Mitchel. Edited by Peter O'Shaughnessy.   Sydney: Kangaroo Press, 1988. 126p. bibliog.

John Mitchel, an Irish intellectual and patriot, spent three years in Van Diemen's Land as a political prisoner. This account of his Tasmanian experience is taken from his much longer book *Jail journal*, published in 1913. The journal distinguishes itself by the quality of the writing and the poetic evocation of the Tasmanian landscape which had escaped the more prosaic chroniclers of Tasmania up to that time. The editor has provided an introduction and explanatory notes.

180   **'To solitude consigned': the Tasmanian journal of William Smith O'Brien 1849-1853. With an introduction to William Smith O'Brien's career, a summary of his voyage to Van Diemen's Land and an epilogue of his last ten years after leaving Tasmania, all by Richard Davis. Also including O'Brien's pocket diaries for 1852 and 1853.**
Edited by Richard Davis and others.   Sydney: Crossing Press, 1995.
484p. maps. bibliog.

William Smith O'Brien was the acknowledged leader of the exiles transported to Van Diemen's Land after conviction for participating in revolution during the Irish struggle for independence in 1848.

181   **The penal settlements of early Van Diemen's Land.**
Thomas James Lempriere.   Hobart: Royal Society of Tasmania (Northern Branch), 1954. 111p.

Having been Commissariat Officer at the penal settlements on Maria Island and then at Macquarie Harbour, Lempriere was appointed in 1839 to Port Arthur and remained there until 1848. Lempriere says in his address to the reader: 'An actual residence in the discharge of his duties, of Ten years, divided between the three Settlements, has naturally given the Author an insight into the peculiarities of each.' A reading of this source document will attest to the truth of this statement.

182 **The journal of Charles O'Hara Booth: Commandant of the Port Arthur penal settlement.**
Edited with an introduction by Dora Heard. Hobart: Tasmanian Historical Research Association, 1981. 298p. bibliog.

O'Hara Booth was commandant of Port Arthur from 1833 to 1844. The journal covers 23 years of his life, from the age of fourteen to thirty-seven. He is seen developing from a light-hearted young officer to the powerful commandant of a large penal settlement. The editor has provided a lengthy, scholarly introduction to the journal.

183 **Port Arthur: a place of misery.**
Maggie Weidenhofer. Port Arthur: B. and M. Reid, in association with Port Arthur Historic Site Management Authority, 1990. 2nd ed. 146p. bibliog.

A detailed, vivid and well-researched account of the famous penal settlement founded in 1830 on Tasman Peninsula in the far south-east of Tasmania. Port Arthur has now attained a new life as a world-wide tourist attraction. [In April 1996 it seemed to revert to its dark past when a lone gunman shot dead 35 and injured 18 tourists in the biggest mass murder in Australia's history.] Many interesting illustrations accompany the text.

184 **Penal peninsula: Port Arthur and its outstations 1827-1898.**
Ian Brand. Launceston: Regal Publications, 1989. Rev. ed. 234p.

A history of the penal establishment of Port Arthur and its outstations on Forester's and Tasman Peninsulas. It is based on documentary material of the period 1827 to 1898, when fires destroyed most of the settlement.

185 **Prison boys of Port Arthur: a study of the Point Puer Boys' Establishment, Van Diemen's Land, 1834 to 1850.**
F. C. Hooper. Melbourne: Cheshire, 1967. 33p.

At Point Puer the boy convicts or 'little depraved felons' were segregated from the main establishment at Port Arthur. This brief account of Point Puer is condensed from Hooper's Master's thesis, *Boys in captivity.*

186 **Escape from Port Arthur.**
Ian Brand. Launceston: Regal Publications, 1991[?]. 63p. maps.

In February 1839 the largest successful escape from Port Arthur penal settlement occurred. Eight convicts escaped in broad daylight. This is the story of their incredible exploit, a 1000-mile journey in an open whale-boat, as told from surviving documents.

187 **The penal settlement of Macquarie Harbour 1822-1833: an outline of its history.**
Hans Julen. Launceston: Royal Publications, 1976. Reprinted 1988. 83p. bibliog.

A short history of the first Van Diemen's Land penal settlement, known to its convict inmates as 'Earthly Hell'. The actual settlement was on Sarah Island. *Sarah Island: an account of the penal settlements of Sarah Island Tasmania, from 1822 to 1833 and 1846-1847* by Ian Brand, which was published in 1984, is another booklet on the subject.

188 Alexander Pearce of Macquarie Harbour: convict – bushranger – cannibal.

Dan Sprod. Hobart: Cat & Fiddle Press, 1977. 173p. bibliog.

The book traces the exploits of the notorious cannibal-convict Alexander Pearce, the Man-Eater of Macquarie Harbour, from his (partly unpublished) confessions to the penal authorities and from various contemporary records. The author separates the truth from sensational legend and examines the factors which motivated Pearce's cannibalism. He also assesses the convict's contribution to the exploration of the wilder regions of the colony.

189 The uncensored story of Martin Cash (Australian bush ranger): as told to James Lester Burke.

Compiled and edited by Joan Dehle Emberg, Buck Thor Emberg. Launceston: Regal Publications, 1991. 268p.

Martin Cash (1810-77) was transported to New South Wales as a convict in 1828 for shooting a rival in love. When pardoned he went to Tasmania where he was convicted again. He escaped from prison several times and pursued a life of bushranging, robbing inns and the houses of rich settlers without undue violence, thus earning the reputation of a 'gentleman bushranger'. He eventually reformed and became a farmer and lived until 1877. Before his death, he told his story to James Lester Burke, an ex-convict and an able writer, who edited the narrative. It was published in Hobart in 1870, and has been reprinted many times since. The present book is published from a transcript of the complete manuscript by Cash, discovered by the editors in the Archives Office of Tasmania. The historical popularizer Frank Clune has published a colourful and fanciful biography of Cash – *Martin Cash: the last of the Tasmanian bushrangers* (1955).

190 The viking of Van Diemen's Land: the stormy life of Jorgen Jorgenson.

Frank Clune, P. R. Stephenson. With illustrations by Albert Zimmerman. Sydney: Angus & Robertson, 1954. 482p. bibliog.

The life of the Scandinavian adventurer Jorgenson, who was in Australian waters during 1802 to 1804 and present at the first settlement on the Derwent in Van Diemen's Land. In 1826 he was sentenced to transportation for life and returned to Van Diemen's Land. After receiving his ticket-of-leave in 1827, he was assigned to the Van Diemen's Land Company and sent to explore parts of the north and north-west of the island. Later he was appointed a convict-constable and employed in the pursuit of Aborigines. After being granted a conditional pardon in 1830, he married and led a dissolute life until his death in 1841. He was a published author and *A shred of autobiography* appeared in two parts in the *Hobart Town Almanack* in 1835 and 1838. A new slightly edited version of this was published by Sullivan's Cove in 1981.

Aborigines

General

191   **The Aboriginal people of Tasmania.**
Julia Clark.   Hobart: Tasmanian Museum and Art Gallery, 1983. 56p.
maps.

An excellent, easily accessible introduction to the Tasmanian Aborigines. Copiously illustrated with contemporary artwork, photographs and, where necessary, by maps and specially drawn diagrams, the book provides ready information about culture, history and race relations with white people.

192   **The Tasmanian Aborigines.**
Brian Plomley.   Launceston: Plomley Foundation, 1993. 107p. maps.
bibliog.

A summary of what is known about the Tasmanian Aborigines today, by an author who has published widely on the subject.

193   **The Aborigines of Tasmania.**
H. Ling Roth.   Hobart: Fuller's Bookshop, 1968. 228p. + 103p. of
appendices. map. bibliog.

This is a facsimile of the second revised and enlarged edition of the book first published in 1899. It is still a useful anthropological study as it brings together the written knowledge about the Tasmanian Aborigines existing at the end of the 19th century.

194   **The Aboriginal Tasmanians.**
Lyndall Ryan.   Brisbane: University of Queensland Press, 1981. 315p.
maps. bibliog.

An excellent, scholarly history of the Tasmanian Aborigines beginning with a
summary of their culture and life before the arrival of the white settlers. The story
continues with an exposition of black–white contact, the resettlement of the
Aborigines on Flinders Island and their life on the island. Finally there is a discussion
of the recent struggles for recognition by their descendants. A fully revised second
edition, which appeared in 1996, brings the Tasmanian Aboriginal story right up to
1995.

195   **Weep in silence: a history of the Flinders Island Aboriginal
settlement, with the Flinders Island journal of George Augustus
Robinson 1835-1839.**
Edited by N. J. B. Plomley.   Hobart: Blubber Head Press, 1987.
1034p. maps. bibliog.

This big book is the sequel to *Friendly mission: the Tasmanian journals and papers of
George Augustus Robinson 1829-1834* (1966). During these five years Robinson
travelled the Tasmanian countryside in search of Aboriginal tribes who were
conducting effective guerrilla warfare against the European settlers. He was successful
in rounding up the remnants of the tribes who were resettled to Flinders Island and
Robinson became Commandant of the Flinders Island Aboriginal settlement. From
1829 to 1839 he kept a detailed journal of his activities and observations of the
Aborigines. The two volumes of transcripts and editor's material have advanced
knowledge of the Aboriginal people of Tasmania to a greater extent than anything else
published so far. A biography of Robinson *Black Robinson: protector of Aborigines*
was published by Vivienne Rae-Ellis in 1988.

196   **Thomas Dove and the Tasmanian Aborigines.**
R. S. Miller. Edited and supplemented by A. M. Harman.   Melbourne:
Spectrum Publications, 1985. 148p. bibliog.

Thomas Dove became Chaplain to the Aboriginal settlement at Wybalenna on Flinders
Island in 1838. The book reveals the problems created by the policy of settling the
remnants of the Tasmanian Aborigine population on Flinders Island. Dove's reports to
the Governor also show the relationships between commandant, chaplain, storekeeper
and other Europeans on the island. Dove left Flinders Island in 1841 and, after being
chaplain to the convicts under the probation system, then held a long ministry at
Swansea from 1844 to 1882.

197   **Jorgen Jorgenson and the Aborigines of Van Diemen's Land:
being a reconstruction of his 'lost' book on their customs and
habits, and on his role in the Roving Parties and the Black Line.**
Edited by N. J. B. Plomley.   Hobart: Blubber Head Press, 1991. 164p.
map. bibliog.

The title of this book is something of a misnomer as only 20 pages refer to the
Aborigines. The rest of the book deals with the Scandinavian adventurer Jorgenson,
George Augustus Robinson, the protector of Aborigines, and the early history of
Tasmania.

198   **The Baudin expedition and the Tasmanian Aborigines 1802.**
       N. J. B. Plomley.   Hobart: Blubber Head Press, 1983. 245p. maps.
       bibliog.

The Frenchmen Nicolas Baudin and François Auguste Peron were leaders of the ninth
party of Europeans to visit southern Tasmania between 1772 and 1802. They were
the last to meet the Aborigines before the English established their first outpost on the
Derwent in 1804. In a superbly produced large-format volume Plomley has edited
the journals, letters and papers of Baudin, Peron and seven others who sailed on the
Géographe and *Naturaliste*. He has collated their observations on Aboriginal society
with material from the earlier French and English expeditions. The text is beautifully
supplemented by the paintings of the expedition's two artists Petit and Lesueur,
reproduced from the collection in the Muséum d'Histoire Naturelle, Le Havre.
Altogether the evidence supports the view that the French were very sympathetic
towards the Aborigines, whereas the English colonists eliminated the native
inhabitants within the first two decades of settling Tasmania.

199   **An officer of the blue: Marc Joseph Marion Dufresne, South Sea**
       explorer 1724-1772.
       Edward Duyker.   Melbourne: Melbourne University Press, 1994.
       229p. bibliog.

Chapter 11, Van Diemen's Land, describes the first contact between white men and
the Tasmanian Aborigines. Tasman, 130 years earlier, had reported only evidence of
fires and notches in trees and heard what was thought to be the distant sound of music.

200   **The demography of hunters and farmers in Tasmania.**
       Rhys Jones.   In: *Aboriginal man and environment in Australia.*
       Edited by D. J. Mulvaney, J. Golson.   Canberra: Australian National
       University Press, 1971, p. 271-287.

This paper compares the populations of the hunters – the Aborigines – and the farmers
– the European settlers – and shows that a population of hunters and gatherers, well
adapted to their environment and established on their land for thousands of years,
collapsed almost at once at their first contact with the farmers. Maps showing tribal
boundaries and the distribution of Aborigines on the island are included, as is a
bibliography.

201   **Tasmanian tribes.**
       Rhys Jones.   In: *Aboriginal tribes of Australia: their terrain,*
       environmental controls, distribution, limits and proper names.
       Norman B. Tindale.   Canberra: Australian National University Press,
       1974, Appendix IX, p. 317-354.

A preliminary archaeological study of the Tasmanian tribes of Aborigines. A detailed,
large-scale map of tribal nomenclature and boundaries is included as well as a
bibliography.

202   **Bruising the red earth: ochre mining and ritual in Aboriginal Tasmania.**
Edited by Antonio Sagona.   Melbourne: Melbourne University Press, 1994. 194p. maps. bibliog.

This is a report, written by specialists, on a multi-disciplinary investigation of the Aboriginal red ochre mine at Toolumbunner, on the southern slopes of the Gog Range in northern Tasmania. It presents an insight into not only the source, extraction and use of ochre, but its significance to Tasmanian Aborigines and other primitive societies in the world.

203   **What the bones say: Tasmanian Aborigines, science, and domination.**
John J. Cove.   Ottawa, Canada: Carlton University Press, 1995. 221p. bibliog.

This scholarly study examines the changing relationship between science and politics with specific reference to indigenous people. The author found that the Tasmanian Aborigines provided the ideal case-study as the victims of cultural genocide who today are involved in political efforts to redress that history and its consequences. The book results from the author's several visits to Tasmania.

204   **Tasmanian Aboriginal language: old and new identities.**
Terry Crowley.   In: *Language and culture in Aboriginal Australia.*
Edited by Michael Walsh, Colin Jallop.   Canberra: Aboriginal Studies Press, 1993, p. 51-71.

This paper argues that 'a separate Tasmanian linguistic identity did not disappear completely with the loss of the original languages, just as the Tasmanian Aborigines themselves did not disappear.'

205   **An annotated bibliography of the Tasmanian Aborigines 1970-1987.**
Claudia Sagona.   Melbourne: Art School Press, Chisholm Institute of Technology, 1989. 290p.

This bibliography is a much expanded and extended edition of N. J. B. Plomley's pioneering work, *An annotated bibliography of the Tasmanian Aborigines* published in 1969, which listed all publications of any consequence concerning the Tasmanian Aborigines up to 1965. The present bibliography is a compilation of books and journal articles written after 1965 and up to 1987, but includes some earlier material not in Plomley's work.

Indigenous viewpoints

206 **Pride against prejudice: reminiscences of a Tasmanian Aborigine.**
Ida West.   Canberra: Australian Institute of Aboriginal Studies, 1987.
Rev. ed. 119p.

The author is a traditional elder of the Aboriginal community in Tasmania. This oral history is of landmark significance, the first time an Aboriginal Tasmanian has told her own story as well as her perception of Tasmanian history and race relations.

207 **The sausage tree.**
Rosalie Medcraft, Valda Gee.   Brisbane: University of Queensland
Press, 1995. 107p.

Childhood reminiscences, set in small-town Tasmania during the Great Depression in the 1930s, written by two Aboriginal sisters, who discovered their black heritage only in adulthood. The book won the 1994 David Unaipon Award for Aboriginal writers.

208 **We who are not here: Aboriginal people of the Huon and Channel today.**
Robyn Friend.   Huonville: Huon Municipal Association, 1992. 132p.

A unique, collective account, in the Aboriginal oral tradition, of the history of the Aboriginal descendants of the Huon Valley region in southern Tasmania. Until recently the existence of a modern Aboriginal community in Tasmania was not recognized, because the last full-bloods had died out in the 19th century.

209 **Weeta Poona: the moon is risen: short stories.**
Jim Everett, Karen Brown. Illustrations by Leigh Maynard, Jim
Everett, Denise Gardner.   Hobart: Tasmanian Aboriginal Centre,
1992. 38p.

A collection of short stories by Tasmania's two best-known Aboriginal writers. In 1992 they published *The spirit of Kuti Kina: Tasmanian Aboriginal poetry.*

Race relations

210 **Fate of a free people.**
Henry Reynolds.   Melbourne: Penguin Books, 1995. 257p. bibliog.

In his previous eight books of history Dr Henry Reynolds has reinterpreted the way in which Australians regard land tenure and their relationship to the original inhabitants – the Aborigines – dispossessed by European settlement. In the present book the author casts his eye on Tasmania and reassesses the black–white conflict in the island state.

211 **Encounters in place: outsiders and Aboriginal Australians 1606-1985.**
D. J. Mulvaney. Brisbane: University of Queensland Press, 1989.
263p. maps. bibliog.

Three chapters are of Tasmanian interest. Chapter 5: *Adventure Bay: a convenient and safe place* in which the author, who is Emeritus Professor of Prehistory at the Australian National University, tells of landings by European explorers at Adventure Bay up to the 1770s. His objective is to analyse these visits as encounters – in terms of diametrically opposed world-views. Chapter 8: *Terror at Cape Grim* relates an Aboriginal massacre by whites at Cape Grim on the north-west tip of Tasmania. Chapter 9: *'Civilized off the face of the Earth' at Wybalama and Oyster Cove* is the story of the last refuge of the full-blood Aborigines.

212 **Community of thieves.**
Cassandra Pybus. Melbourne: Heinemann, 1991. 198p. maps. bibliog.

This is a lively, readable and sad story of black–white relations in Tasmania. It is concerned with the dispossession of the Aborigines. The author, a fifth-generation Tasmanian, explores her family's past and tries to face up personally to her responsibilities in the present for the destruction of Aboriginal society in the island state.

213 **Trucanini: queen or traitor.**
Vivienne Rae-Ellis. Canberra: Australian Institute of Aboriginal Studies, 1981. New, expanded ed. 194p. bibliog.

A biography of 'Queen Trucanini' (1812-76), the Tasmanian Aboriginal woman who became known as 'the last Tasmanian'. The author, who has published other books about Tasmania, describes the drama of Trucanini's life against the background of violence and disruption imposed on the Aboriginal tribes of Tasmania by the English invasion at the beginning of the 19th century. This new edition of the book, first published in 1976, includes additional material; an account of land rights claims, as well as a number of new illustrations of Trucanini and other Tasmanians of her generation. A fictional account, co-authored by Rae-Ellis and Nancy Cato, *Queen Trucanini*, was published in 1976.

214 **Black war: the extermination of the Tasmanian Aborigines.**
Clive Turnbull, with an introduction by H. Ian Hogbin. Melbourne: Cheshire, 1948. 274p. bibliog.

A pioneering investigation into the genocide of Aborigines in Tasmania during the first generation of English settlement. The book has been reprinted several times, the last in a paperback edition by Sun Books in 1974.

215 **The Tasmanians: the story of a doomed race.**
Robert Travers. Melbourne: Cassell, 1968. 244p. bibliog.

This is the story of the extermination of the full-blood Aboriginal Tasmanians within a single generation of English settlement of the island.

Religion

216 **The Anglican Church in Tasmania: a diocesan history to mark the sesquicentenary 1992.**
Geoffrey Stephens. Hobart: Trustees of the Diocese, 1991. 272p.
A history of the largest church in Tasmania. According to official statistics just over 40 per cent of Tasmanians are affiliated with the Anglican Church. The next biggest – the Catholic Church – lays claim to 22 per cent of the population.

217 **History of the Church of England in Tasmania.**
W. R. Barrett. Hobart: 'The Mercury' Press, 1942. 92p.
Published to commemorate the 100th anniversary of the foundation of the diocese of Tasmania. There is no acknowledgement of sources used and no index, although judging from the wealth of detail in the text, Church records must have been consulted, as well as the *Year book of the Church of England in the Diocese of Tasmania*, first published in 1891.

218 **The pioneer bishop in Van Diemen's Land 1843-1863: letters and memories of Francis Russell Nixon D.D., first Bishop of Tasmania.**
Collected and compiled by Norah Nixon. Hobart: Walch, 1953. 64p.
An introduction to the first Church of England Bishop of Tasmania, and his family, through letters written by his wife, Anna Maria, to her father and relatives in England, and in later years letters written by the Bishop himself. They are personal and intimate, but give a vivid picture of their home life and reveal the hardships and problems of the early days of the colony and the Diocese of Tasmania.

219 **Knopwood: a biography.**
Geoffrey Stephens. Hobart: The Author, 1990. 226p. bibliog.
The Reverend Robert Knopwood arrived in Van Diemen's Land with David Collins's expedition in 1804 to set up the foundation settlement at Hobart Town. From 1803 he had begun to keep a diary which he continued until his death in 1838. The diary was

50

published in a scholarly edition by the Tasmanian Historical Research Associated in 1977 – *The diary of the Reverend Robert Knopwood 1803-1838: first chaplain of Van Diemen's Land* – and is important for shedding light on life in the young colony at a time from which few personal records exist. Besides being Chaplain, Knopwood also acted as magistrate for many years. The biography shows him as a typical sporting parson of kindly disposition and fond of conviviality. A summary of the more important parts of the diary can be found in *An introduction to the diaries of the Rev. Robert Knopwood, A. M. and G. T. W. B. Boyes*, by Wilfrid Hugh Hudspeth, published by the Royal Society of Tasmania in 1954.

220   **Planting a faith in Tasmania: the country parishes.**
      W. T. Southerwood.   Hobart: [n.p.], 1977. 237p. bibliog.
This eighth and final volume in the Planting a Faith series brings to a conclusion the story of the Catholic Church in Tasmania. The other titles concerned (among other topics): the Catholic parishes in Hobart, Launceston, Queenstown and Tasmania's north-west. All are written by Father Southerwood.

221   **Women of faith and action: history of the Catholic Women's League, Tasmania 1941-1986.**
      Anne Rushton Nuss.   Hobart: Southern Holdings for the Catholic Women's League, Tasmania, 1986. 127p.
A celebratory, uncritical rendition of the first 45 years of the League.

222   **William Hutchins: the first Archdeacon of Van Diemen's Land 1792-1841.**
      D. B. Clarke.   Hobart: Speciality Press, 1986. 143p. bibliog.
This biography is adapted from the author's doctoral thesis and is published to mark the 150th anniversary of the Archdeaconate of Hutchins. His name lives on in the Hutchins School in Hobart, one of Australia's great schools, from which the author retired as headmaster shortly before the book`'s publication. The book covers an important time in Tasmania's history, a period during which important matters concerning Church and State, and the State's role in education were being settled.

223   **The convicts' friend: a life of Bishop Robert William Willson, Apostle to prisoners and the insane in the Australian colonies of Tasmania, Victoria and New South Wales.**
      W. T. Southerwood.   George Town: Stella Maris Books, 1989. 424p. bibliog.
A biography of R. W. Willson who became the first Bishop of Hobart Town when he arrived from England in 1844. Besides being a clergyman, he was a social reformer much concerned with the welfare of convicts and the mentally handicapped. Thus the book is a good source for the social conditions prevailing in Tasmania during his period in office which ended with is death in 1866.

224 The wisdom of Guilford Young.

W. T. Southerwood. George Town: Stella Maris Books, 1988. 752p.

A lengthy biography of Sir Guilford Young, Archbishop of Hobart from 1955 until his death in 1988. Written by Father Southerwood, the author of several books about the Catholic Church in Tasmania, the book shows that Young not only exercised great influence within the Church, but also took sometimes controversial attitudes in Tasmania's public life.

225 Presbyterian Church of Tasmania: triple jubilee 1973.

Record compiled and edited by R. S. Miller. Photography by W. R. Harvey. Hobart: Presbytery of Tasmania, 1973. 130p.

Updates the history of the Presbyterian Church in Tasmania since the publication of the Rev. J. Heyer's definitive study, *The Presbyterian pioneers of Van Diemen's Land*, which was published in 1935 (see item no. 226). The emphasis is therefore on developments in the Church during the years 1935 to 1973.

226 The Presbyterian pioneers of Van Diemen's Land: a contribution to the ecclesiastical history of Tasmania.

J. Heyer. Launceston: Presbytery of Tasmania, 1935. 270p.

A history of the Presbyterian Church in Tasmania, published to commemorate the centenary of its establishment.

227 Congregationalism in Tasmania 1830-1977: a brief history.

Compiled by Theo. E. Sharples. Hobart: Congregational Union of Tasmania, 1977. 70p. map. bibliog.

A history of Congregationalism in Tasmania before amalgamation in 1977 with the Methodists and Presbyterians to become the Uniting Church in Australia.

228 A chronicle of Methodism in Van Diemen's Land 1820-1840.

Compiled by R. D. Pretyman. Melbourne: The Aldersgate Press, 1970. 128p. bibliog.

A history of the establishment of Methodism in Tasmania based on original sources and published to commemorate the sesquicentenary of Methodism in Tasmania. Methodists joined with the Congregational and Presbyterian Churches in 1976 to form the Uniting Church. A short booklet, *Tasmanian Methodism 1820-1975*, was issued at that time, outlining the development of the Church throughout Tasmania.

229 Baptists in Van Diemen's Land: the story of Tasmania's first Baptist church, the Hobart Town Particular Baptist Chapel, Harrington Street, 1835-1886.

Laurence F. Rowston. Launceston and Hobart: The Baptist Union of Tasmania and The Hobart Baptist Church, 1985. 120p. bibliog.

Published on the occasion of the sesquicentenary of the constitution of the first Baptist church in the Australian colonies, this is a well-researched study of the origins of the Baptist Church in Tasmania. It is also an account of the life and career of the Revd Henry Dowling, Van Diemen's Land's first Baptist minister.

230   One hundred years of witness: a history of the Hobart Baptist Church 1884-1984.
Laurence F. Rowston.   Hobart: Hobart Baptist Church, 1984. 75p.
A straightforward chronological account of the contributions of various Baptist leaders and pastors in Hobart.

231   Mission to the islands: the missionary voyages in Bass Strait of Canon Marcus Brownrigg 1872-1885.
Edited with an introduction by Stephen Murray-Smith.   Hobart: Cat & Fiddle Press, 1979. 246p. maps. bibliog.
In the 1830s the islands of Bass Strait were the institutionalized exile for the Aborigines rounded up in Tasmania, most of whom had perished by 1847. However, European sealers had plied their trade here since 1797 and had cohabited with Aboriginal women, thus creating a half-caste race which still exists today. This book presents the edited accounts of missionary visits to the islands to service the population between 1872 and 1885. The editor also supplies a lucid introduction and a biographical list with vital details of the most important people from the islands.

232   Henry Reed, Van Diemen's Land pioneer.
Hudson Fysh.   Hobart: Cat & Fiddle Press, 1973. 159p. bibliog.
A biography of Henry Reed (1806-80), businessman, philanthropist and fervent Christian evangelist, written by his grandson, one of the founders of Qantas airline. The book throws light also on the early settlement of Tasmania.

233   The history of the Church of Jesus Christ of Latter-Day Saints: Tasmania 1854-1992.
Preben Villy Scott, Donald Arthur Woolley.   Ulverstone: The Authors, 1993. 263p.
This story of the Mormons in Tasmania has been compiled from original records when they have been available. Otherwise it relies on the memories of members of the Church.

234   Churches of Van Diemen's Land.
Reg A. Watson.   Hobart: O.B.M. Publishing Department, 1976. 56p.
A presentation of short histories of church buildings dating from the 1820s and scattered throughout Tasmania. Many of the buildings are illustrated with drawings by Edna Sackett.

Society

235 Life in Van Diemen's Land.
Joan Goodrick.   Adelaide: Rigby, 1980. 220p.

An easy-to-read, popular history of the first half-century of European settlement in Tasmania. It is mainly concerned with the daily lives of free settlers, the poorer o whom led lives of great hardship. A similar popular book of historical anecdotes i Coultman Smith's *Tales of old Tasmania*, published in 1978.

236 Launceston talks: oral histories of the Launceston community.
Edited by Jill Cassidy, Elspeth Wishart. Interviews conducted by Jill Cassidy. Photographic portraits by Brian Allison.   Launceston: Regal Publications, 1990. 178p.

The Launceston Bicentennial Oral History Project was carried out by the Queer Victoria Museum and Art Gallery in 1988-89 as a means of involving the community in the recording of Launceston's history. The interviews, which appear in the book are restricted to nine areas, either relating to historical events, such as the 1929 floods and World War II; or, to major industries such as the railway workshops, the textile factories and vehicle manufacturing in the 1930s; or, to social groups such as the Chinese. Altogether the book provides an insight into Launceston's social history through the eyes of ordinary people.

237 Valley people.
Jim Marwood.   Sydney: Kangaroo Press, 1984. 144p. map.

A record, in photographs and words, of the way of life of a small group of people who live in the Fingal Valley in eastern Tasmania. The people, interviewed by the author, belong to the generation whose memories go back to the beginning of the twentieth century and the book captures vividly the everyday events and attitudes of yesterday.

238   **The pink triangle: the gay law reform debate in Tasmania.**
Miranda Morris.   Sydney: University of New South Wales Press,
1995. 134p. bibliog.
The debate about Tasmania's repressive homosexuality laws began in 1988 and
eventually led to the intervention of the United Nations Human Rights Committee.
The author presents both sides of the argument on homosexuality reform in a readable
manner. As a result she raises interesting questions about Tasmanian society in
comparison to the rest of Australia.

239   **A divided society: Tasmania during World War I.**
Marilyn Lake.   Melbourne: Melbourne University Press, 1975. 213p.
bibliog.
Describes the impact of World War I on the Tasmanian community and demonstrates
people's different perceptions of the nature and importance of the war. Far from being
a unifying influence, the author is convinced that 'the effect of the impact of war was
not a welding together but a disintegration, a fragmentation of the community. The
forces which divided men had not lessened, but strengthened. Class was set against
class, creed against creed, district against district, soldier against civilian.'

240   **Bushfire disaster: an Australian community in crisis.**
R. L. Wettenhall.   Sydney: Angus & Robertson, 1975. 320p. maps.
bibliog.
On 7 February 1967 a bushfire which had started in the surrounding countryside
invaded Hobart, the capital of Tasmania, and within hours caused the deaths of 62
persons and the destruction of 1300 houses and other property adding up to a damage
bill of many millions of dollars. Dr Wettenhall analyses the disaster, in which he was
involved, against the background of disasters in Australia in general and draws
conclusions about the need for preparedness and community organization in the event
of emergencies. The text is complemented with dramatic photographs of the effect of
the fire.

241   **Prostitution in Tasmania during the transition from penal
settlement to 'civilised' society.**
In: *So much hard work: women and prostitution in Australian history.*
Edited by Kay Daniels.   Sydney: Fontana/Collins, 1984, p. 15-86.
A scholarly history of prostitution in Tasmania during the 19th century.

242   **Governors' ladies: the wives and mistresses of Van Diemen's Land
governors.**
Alison Alexander.   Hobart: Tasmanian Historical Research
Association, 1987. 188p. bibliog.
The author, a historian, describes a group of women connected with various
Tasmanian governors, either as mistresses or as wives. On a broader scale the book is
a good reflection of a colonial society's changing expectations of women.

243   **The Tasmanian Club 1861-1961.**
      Frank C. Green.   Hobart: The Club, 1961. 93p.

Founded in the British tradition as a Gentlemen's club, the Tasmanian Club has been a venue for the establishment to the present day. A similar club was formed in 1894 in Launceston. Its story is told by Raymond Ferrall in *The story of the Northern Club, 1894-1994.*

244   **The history of scouting in Tasmania 1909-1985.**
      Ray Jeffrey.   Hobart: The Scout Association of Australia, Tasmanian Branch, 1990. 248p.

The story of scouting in Tasmania, from its beginnings in the early years of this century to the present.

245   **Atlas of the Australian people: Tasmania, 1986 Census.**
      Prepared by Graeme Hugo, with the assistance of the Bureau of Immigration Research.   Canberra: Australian Government Publishing Service, 1989. 371p. maps. bibliog.

Documents the diverse ethnic characteristics of the population and the changing spatial distribution of first- and second-generation immigrants to Tasmania. The research is based upon the data of the 1986 population census. The first volume of the 1991 series of volumes *Atlas of the Australian people – 1991 Census: national overview* was published in 1995 and is to be followed by the individual state volumes, including Tasmania.

246   **The hand of friendship: a history of the Good Neighbour Council of Tasmania 1949-1992.**
      Gillian Winter.   Hobart: Good Neighbour Council of Tasmania, 1993. 94p. bibliog.

The Good Neighbour Council of Tasmania was established by the Federal Government as part of its plan for a national Good Neighbour Movement. The Movement was designed to welcome and help migrants who arrived in large numbers after the Second World War as part of a new and ambitious immigration programme.

247   **The Monument of Polish–Australian Brotherhood-in-Arms.**
      Edited by Tadeusz Kempa.   Hobart: T. Kempa, Tasmania Polonia's Fund and Peter Polacik, 1984. 189p.

This book was compiled for the occasion of unveiling the Monument of Polish–Australian Brotherhood-in-Arms, which coincided with the 30th anniversary of the Polish Association in Hobart. The book gives some of the background of the Monument but for the greater part its contents relate to the activities of the Polish community in Tasmania and elsewhere in Australia.

248 **Jews in Van Diemen's Land.**
Max Gordon. Melbourne: Ponsford Newman & Benson, 1965. 141p.
bibliog.
The story of Jewish convicts and settlers in Tasmania up to the 120th anniversary celebrations of the laying of the foundation stone of the Hobart Synagogue on 9 August 1963.

249 **Landfall in Van Diemen's Land: the Steels' quest for greener pastures.**
Gwyneth and Hume Dow. Melbourne: Footprint, 1990. 196p.
Essentially a family history, based on a bundle of letters written home to England by those members of the Steel family who had migrated to and settled in Van Diemen's Land. The joint authors focus on the paths of the settlers towards wealth and hoped-for gentility, thus providing a mirror on colonial society. The book contains valuable material for the economic and social historian.

Health and Welfare

250 **Portrait of a hospital: the Royal Hobart.**
W. G. Rimmer. Hobart: Royal Hobart Hospital, 1981. 328p. bibliog.
A detailed history of the hospital from its foundation as a convict institution in 1803 to 1980. The text is supplemented with black-and-white illustrations.

251 **Launceston General Hospital: first hundred years 1863-1963.**
Clifford Craig. Launceston: Board of Management of the Launceston General Hospital, 1963. 138p.
Dr Craig was associated with the hospital in various capacities since he first arrived in 1926 as surgeon-superintendent. He retired in 1961. The book is mainly based on his recollections of that period. There are many black-and-white photographs.

252 **A century of caring: Latrobe's Hospital 1887-1987. An illustrated history of the Devon Cottage Hospital, the Devon Public Hospital and the Mersey General Hospital in Northern Tasmania.**
John R. Wilson. Latrobe: Graduate Nurses' Association Centennial Celebrations Committee, Mersey General Hospital, Latrobe, Tasmania, 1988. 306p. maps.
A centenary history of the hospital at Latrobe on the Mersey River in northern Tasmania south of Devonport. The text is supplemented with many illustrations.

253 **Troubled asylum: the history of the . . . Royal Derwent Hospital.**
R. W. Gowlland. New Norfolk: Royal Derwent Hospital, 1981. 200p. maps.
Established in 1827, the Royal Derwent Hospital was at the time of the book's publication the oldest psychiatric hospital in Australia still standing on its original site.

254 **Pills, potions and politics: the formation of the Pharmaceutical Society of Tasmania 1886-1891.**
Jillian Finch.   Hobart: The Pharmaceutical Society of Australia (Tasmanian Branch), 1991. 88p. bibliog.
A well-researched history of the founding of the Pharmaceutical Society of Tasmania, the book also casts new light on the general state of medical care in Tasmania during the 1880s.

255 **'Outpost medicine': Australasian studies on the history of medicine.**
Edited by Susanne Atkins and others.   Hobart: University of Tasmania and the Australian Society of the History of Medicine, 1994. 412p. bibliog.
This volume contains the papers presented at the Third National Conference of the Australian Society of the History of Medicine held in Hobart in February 1993. Several of the papers presented are of Tasmanian interest.

256 **Sanatorium of the South? Public health and politics in Hobart and Launceston 1875-1914.**
Stefan Petrow.   Hobart: Tasmanian Historical Research Association, 1995. 218p. bibliog.
Based on the author's Master of Arts thesis the 'book considers how the Hobart and Launceston municipal councils shouldered their responsibilities in the crucial area of public health when faced with a series of epidemics in the late nineteenth and early twentieth centuries.'

257 **The great scourge: the Tasmanian infantile paralysis epidemic 1937-1938.**
Anne Killalea.   Hobart: Tasmanian Historical Research Association, 1995. 165p. map. bibliog.
An investigation of the poliomyelitis epidemic in Tasmania in 1937/38, the largest per caput epidemic of polio the Western world has ever seen, or would see again. The book began as a Master of Humanities thesis, History Department, University of Tasmania, 1992. It appears here with alterations, and the addition of photographs.

258 **Dr William Paton 1800-1854: a colonial surgeon in Van Diemen's Land.**
Jeffrey R. Briscoe.   Hobart: Strawberry Press, 1991. 263p. bibliog.
Describing the life of a doctor in early Van Diemen's Land, the book provides an insight into the life of the developing colony due to the wide interests of Paton. He was well known during his lifetime as a talented medico, a landowner, a local magistrate, a confidant of Government officials, a popular lecturer, secretary and chairman of countless local committees.

259   **'Poverty is not a crime': the development of social services in Tasmania 1803-1900.**
   Joan C. Brown.   Hobart: Tasmanian Historical Research Association, 1972. 192p. bibliog.

The book is based on the author's Master of Arts thesis. It outlines the social services provided by government and voluntary agencies in the state from white settlement in 1803 to the time of federation. The author also examines community attitudes towards the poor and afflicted, and the attitudes and actions of various colonial authorities towards the underprivileged.

260   **With skill and dedication: the development of volunteer town fire brigades in Tasmania.**
   Roger V. McNeice.   Hobart: Tasmania Fire Service, 1993. 516p. bibliog.

This large-format volume is McNeice's fourth on Tasmanian fire brigades. The centenary of the Hobart Fire Brigade was celebrated in 1983 with the publication of *Helmets and hatchets: a history of the Hobart Fire Brigade 1883-1983. Men of fire: a history of the Launceston Fire Brigade* appeared in 1987 and was followed in 1991 by *Knapsack heroes: Tasmania's country fire brigades in action.* All four books are copiously illustrated and all were published by the Tasmania Fire Service. The author has been involved with fire brigades since 1968 and writes from personal experience.

Politics and Government

261 **The government of Tasmania.**
W. A. Townsley.   Brisbane: University of Queensland Press, 1976.
169p. bibliog.
This book is part of a series, Governments of the Australian states and territories,
which deals with the politics and administration of the states and territories. Professor
Townsley explores the effects of social, geographical and economic factors on the
island state's political system.

262 **A century of responsible government 1856-1956.**
Edited by F. C. Green.   Hobart: L. G. Shea, Government Printer,
1956. 317p.
The greater portion of the book is taken up by an essay by Professor W. A. Townsley
in which he reviews the development and working of government in Tasmania during
its first 100 years. The book also includes chapters with brief biographical notes about
premiers, political leaders, and Speakers of the House of Assembly and Presidents of
the Legislative Council.

263 **The price of power: the politics behind the Tasmanian dams case.**
Doug Lowe.   Melbourne: Macmillan, 1984. 184p.
The struggle from the late 1970s on to 1983 to save the south-west wilderness area of
Tasmania from the construction of a dam on the Gordon River, below the Franklin,
was one of the great conservation battles of the world. Doug Lowe was Premier of
Tasmania during this time and on 11 November 1981 was deposed as leader of the
pro-dam Parliamentary Labor Party. This book presents a lucid and remarkably
objective account of the political events by the principal role-player in the drama.

264 **The Tasmanian parliamentary Accord and public policy 1989-92: accommodating the new politics?**
Edited by Marcus Howard, Peter Larmour.   Canberra: Federalism Research Centre, The Australian National University, 1993. 220p. bibliogs.

The Tasmanian election of May 1989, which saw the election of five Green Independents to the House of Assembly, led to a unique arrangement in Australian politics. The minority Australian Labor Party (ALP) government was commissioned on the basis of a written agreement, rather than a coalition, between the ALP and the Greens. The Accord, as it became known, collapsed in October 1990 although the ALP remained in government until its defeat in an election in February 1992. This edited volume of papers by specialists in their fields, examines the impact of minority government and Green politics on public policy in Tasmania.

265 **A guide to Tasmanian government administration.**
R. L. Wettenhall.   Hobart: Platypus Publications, 1968. 341p. maps. bibliog.

The author classifies and describes the various departments, commissions and instrumentalities which have proliferated in Tasmania in over a century of responsible government. It is primarily a reference work covering the whole state administration.

266 **A bibliography of literature on Tasmanian politics and government.**
Dora Heard, Ralph J. K. Chapman.   Hobart: University of Tasmania, 1974. 32p.

This first-ever general bibliography on Tasmanian politics appeared as a separate supplement to the journal of the Australasian Political Studies Association – *Politics*, vol. 8, no. 1, May 1974.

267 **The Parliament of Tasmania: an historical sketch.**
Carrel Inglis Clark.   Hobart: Government Printer, 1947. 88 + 30p.

A history of the Tasmanian parliament by the then clerk of the Legislative Council. Part II, paged separately, contains a record of the services of members and officers of the Legislative Council and the House of Assembly since the introduction of responsible government in 1856.

268 **Representation of the Tasmanian people: expanded edition 1803-1994.**
Terry Newman.   Hobart: Tasmanian Parliamentary Library, 1994. 239p. maps. bibliog.

Supersedes the first edition of this work which appeared in 1985. This edition has been comprehensively revised, eliminating errors and updating information to early 1994. Much of the information is set out in tabular form for easy reference, such as election results, elected representatives and office bearers of the parliament. Both the state and national parliaments are covered. This is an indispensable reference for the political scientist and historian. A pamphlet on *Referenda in Tasmania* was published in 1984.

269   **Hare-Clark in Tasmania: representations of all opinions.**
Terry Newman.   Hobart: Joint Library Committee of the Parliament
of Tasmania, 1992. 319p.

The Hare-Clark system of proportional representation has been used in Tasmanian
elections since 1909. This book is the definitive work on the subject.

270   **On the brink: the Denison pre-election survey.**
In: *Labor to power: Australia's 1972 election.*   Edited by Henry
Mayer.   Sydney: Angus & Robertson on behalf of the Australasian
Political Studies Association, 1973, p. 128-135.

This is very probably the only voter survey in a Tasmanian electorate in existence. It
surveys voters in the seat of Denison before the historic 1972 federal election, when
the Australian Labor Party was voted into power after 23 years of rule by the Liberal
Party of Australia. The survey is immediately followed by an interesting chapter,
Defeat in Denison, written by Dr R. J. Solomon, the previous Liberal member of
parliament, giving reasons for his defeat.

271   **Eighty years Labor: the ALP in Tasmania 1903-1983.**
Richard Davis.   Hobart: Sassafras Books and the History Department,
University of Tasmania, 1983. 163p. bibliog.

A history of the Australian Labor Party in Tasmania. It has an exceptional record in
the island state – at the time of publication of this book – 52 years in government
during a total life of 80 years.

272   **Tasmania.**
R. P. Davis.   In: *Labor in politics: the state labor parties in Australia.*
Edited by D. J. Murphy.   Brisbane: University of Queensland Press,
1975, p. 389-444.

Traces the emergence and development of the labour movement as a political force in
Tasmania between 1880 and 1920.

273   **Tasmania: premiers and parochial politics.**
Richard Davis.   In: *Machine politics in the Australian Labor Party.*
Edited by Andrew Parkin, John Warhurst.   Sydney: Allen & Unwin,
1983, p. 186-209.

An analysis of the internal politics in the Tasmanian Branch of the Australian Labor
Party.

274   **Labor in Lyons: the Wilmot-Lyons story to celebrate the Labor
centenary 1891-1991.**
Compiled by Dorothy Sherry and others.   Devonport: Lyons
Electorate Council of the A.L.P., 1991. 126p. maps. bibliog.

Of the five electorates of Tasmania Wilmot, renamed Lyons in 1984, is by far the
largest, comprising roughly half of the state and it is the most varied electorate. This
history has been written by ordinary members of the Australian Labor Party in an

attempt 'to give the reader a better understanding of the history of Federal and State Labor politics and politicans and how it has affected the Wilmot-Lyons electorate over the past century.' All statistics of election results and other details are based on official records.

275 I had 50,000 bosses: memoirs of a Labor backbencher 1946-1975.
Gil Duthie.   Sydney: Angus & Robertson, 1984. 366p.

Gil Duthie represented the electorate of Wilmot, Tasmania, in the federal parliament in Canberra for 29 years. This is a personal account of what makes a Member of Parliament tick and provides insights of federal electoral politics in Tasmania.

276 King O'Malley: 'the American bounder'.
A. R. Hoyle.   Melbourne: Macmillan, 1981. 186p. bibliog.

Born in North America, King O'Malley came to Australia in 1888. After a chequered career selling insurance and speculating in property both in Tasmania and on the mainland, in 1901 he became a Member of the first Commonwealth Parliament, representing the north-west of Tasmania. He was re-elected and represented this electorate until 1917. For a time from 1910 he was Minister for Home Affairs. O'Malley was a flamboyant character and myths, to which he generously contributed, abounded about him during his lifetime. This book is to some extent a debunking biography.

277 The Tasmanian division.
In: *Power in the Liberal Party: a study in Australian politics.*
Katharine West.   Melbourne: Cheshire, 1965, p. 187-209.

Chapter 6 is concerned with the Tasmanian division of the Liberal Party of Australia, which despite its name represents the conservative interests in the country. The book is not concerned with the Party's formal structure (which is outlined in the Appendix), but with the actual location of power in the Party and with the nature of power relations within it.

278 So we take comfort.
Dame Enid Lyons.   London: Heinemann, 1965. 283p.

This is an account of the author's life with J. A. Lyons, Premier of Tasmania and later Prime Minister of Australia from 1932 to 1939, in which year he died. They were both born in Tasmania. Dame Enid became a Member of the Commonwealth Parliament in 1943, representing the Tasmanian seat of Darwin, which she held until 1951. During these years she became the first woman Minister in federal political history. Her experiences as a woman politician are described in *Among the carrion crows*, published in 1972. A third-hand account of the Lyons's relationship can be found in Kate White's *A political love story: Joe and Enid Lyons*, published in 1987.

279 **Prelude to federation (1884-1898): extracts from the journal of James Backhouse Walker F.R.G.S., legal practitioner, historian, author.**
Edited by Peter Benson Walker. Hobart: O.B.M. Publishing Company, 1976. 199p. bibliog.
This book contains extracts from the journals of James Backhouse Walker, 'a founding father of serious Tasmanian historical studies and writing'. It recounts in terse, vivid language the major political issues of the day, leading up to the plebiscite for Federation in 1898.

280 **The life and times of Sir Richard Dry: eminent Tasmanian statesman. First native-born Premier and Speaker of the House of Assembly in the Parliament of Tasmania 1815-1869.**
A. D. Baker. Hobart: Oldham, Beddome & Meredith, 1951. 110p.
Dry was one of the most popular and esteemed public men of his time. Besides being an account of his life, the book is also a study of Tasmania during his lifetime.

281 **The Whitehead letters: Tasmanian society and politics 1871-1882 as seen through the letter-books of John Whitehead MHA of 'Winburn', Lymington.**
Compiled by Francesca A. Vernon. Edited by Michael N. Sprod. Hobart: Tasmanian Historical Research Association, 1991. 270p. map. bibliog.
Whitehead was a landowner and member of parliament from 1869 to 1880. His letters written to a friend in England reveal a conservative private view of farming matters and social and political life in Tasmania from the 1870s and early 1880s, a neglected period in Tasmanian historiography.

282 **Mr Punch in Tasmania: colonial politics in cartoons, 1866-1879.**
Clifford Craig. Hobart: Blubber Head Press, 1980. 311p. bibliog.
Between 1866 and 1879 Tasmania sustained no less than six imitations of the successful London *Punch* magazine. The book reproduces virtually all full-page cartoons with accompanying text. It also povides a history of each of the six journals and gathers information on owners, editors, artists and contributors. Altogether it gives a rich commentary on Tasmanian political and social life in the second half of the 19th century. In addition it makes a valuable contribution to the history of black-and-white art in the colony.

Law and Order

283 **An Australian legal history.**
  Alex C. Castles.   Sydney: Law Book Company, 1982. 553p.
Until separation from New South Wales in 1824 the law of New South Wales applied
in Van Diemen's Land. Chapter 11: Van Diemen's Land 1824-1850, traces the
differences which emerged between the working of the law in the two colonies after
separation. There are other textual references to Tasmania throughout the book, and
these are easily identifiable from the table of contents, the table of cases and that of
statutes, as well as the index.

284 **The Tasmanian law handbook.**
  Hobart Community Legal Service.   Hobart: The Service, 1994.
  2nd ed. 1134p.
This practical guide to over 30 different areas of law, written by experts in their field,
is a comprehensive guide to the legal system as it operates in Tasmania.

285 **The brief case: a collection of papers on Tasmanian legal**
  memorabilia and Tasmanian places associated with the 21st
  Australian Legal Convention.
  Compiled by George Deas Brown, Peter Benson Walker for the Law
  Council of Australia.   Hobart: Melanie Publications, 1981. 90p.
  bibliog.
Contains short articles on the law and some of its prominent practitioners in Tasmania.

286 **Court in the colony: Hobart Town May, 1824.**
  Edited by J. N. D. Harrison.   Hobart: Law Society of Tasmania, 1974.
  44p.
This booklet was produced by the Law Society of Tasmania to mark the
sesquicentenary of the opening of the Supreme Court of Tasmania on 10 May 1824. It

is not a sustained exposition of the history of the law, or of lawyers in the state, but a personalized collection of memoirs, vignettes and sketches, contributed by practising lawyers.

287 **History and status of the legal profession: being the text of two lectures delivered in the Law School of the University of Tasmania on the 12th and 15th June 1967.**
Peter Crisp. Hobart: University of Tasmania, 1968. 36p.
A short account of the history and status of the legal profession set in the context of the development of the British system.

288 **The South West Dam dispute: the legal and political issues: a collection of essays presented at seminars at the Law School, University of Tasmania.**
Edited by M. Sornarajah. Hobart: Sir Elliott Lewis Memorial Publication, University of Tasmania, 1983. 151p. bibliogs.
These seminars on the legal issues arising from the dispute were arranged while the South West Dam case was before the High Court of Australia.

289 **Sir John Pedder: first Chief Justice of Tasmania.**
J. M. Bennett. Hobart: University of Tasmania, 1977. 47p. biblog.
Pedder was Chief Justice of Tasmania from 1824 when it became a separate colony from New South Wales, until his resignation in 1854. This biography is also a valuable source of the early legal history of Tasmania and of colonial history in general.

290 **The Franklin Dam case.**
Commentary by Michael Coper, and full text of the decision in Commonwealth of Australia v. State of Tasmania. Sydney: Butterworths, 1983. 26p. + p. 625-867.
The Franklin Dam case was one of the most important constitutional law decisions since the creation of the federal system of government in Australia. This book is based on the full text, headnote and summary of the case as presented in Volume 46 of the *Australian Law Reports*. To this material Coper has added an extensive commentary designed to clarify the issues and questions raised by the High Court decision. There is a detailed index to the text of the decision and the commentary.

291 **Legal research: material and methods.**
Enid Campbell and others. Sydney: Law Book Company, 1988. 3rd ed. 326p. bibliogs.
A guide to publications such as statutes, parliamentary papers, government publications, law reports and others useful in conducting legal research. Each kind of publication and institution is treated under separate sections for each state and territory. Thus the reader looks to Tasmania in either the table of contents or the index.

292 Mounted police of Victoria and Tasmania.

John O'Sullivan.   Adelaide: Rigby, 1980. 211p. bibliog.

Part 3 of the book describes the development of the mounted police in Tasmania from the early 19th century to the late 1930s when horses were abandoned and the police were equipped with motorcycles.

293 The Tasmanian gallows: a study of capital punishment.

Richard P. Davis.   Hobart: Cat & Fiddle Press, 1974. 119p. bibliog.

This is the story of the death penalty in Tasmania, from the colony's establishment as a penal colony in 1803 to the abolition of capital punishment in 1968.

294 Brady, McCabe, Dunne, Bryan, Crawford, Murphy, Bird, McKenney, Goodwin, Pawley, Bryant, Cody, Hodgetts, Gregory, Tilley, Ryan, Williams and their associates: bushrangers in Van Diemen's Land 1824-1827.

From James Calder's text of 1873, together with newly discovered manuscripts, edited by Eustace Fitzsymonds.   Adelaide: Sullivan's Cove, 1979. 180p. map.

A reprint of James Calder's lively account of *Brady, the first troubles of Governor Arthur*, first printed in the Hobart *Mercury* during August 1873 with copious manuscript material from various repositories, transcribed and interpolated into Calder's original text. Readers may also wish to consult James Bonwick's *The bushrangers: illustrating the early days of Van Diemen's Land*, originally published in 1856 and issued in facsimile in 1967.

Military History

295 Tasmania's war effort: Australia remembers 1945-1995.
Written and compiled by Matt O'Brien. Hobart: Department of
Premier and Cabinet, 1995. 111p.

A new edition of a book first published in 1946 to put on record Tasmania's
contribution to Australia's war effort during World War II.

296 Tasmania's war record 1914-1918.
Edited by L. Broinowski. Hobart: J. Walch, for the Government of
Tasmania, 1921. 370p.

The official record of the contribution of Tasmania and Tasmanians to the war effort
during World War I. The history of one particular unit of the Australian Imperial
Force is told by F. C. Green in *The Fortieth: a record of the 40th Battalion, A.I.F.*,
published in 1922.

297 Tasmanians in the Transvaal War.
John Bufton. Hobart: Loone, 1905. 534p.

During the Boer War of 1899 to 1902, the Australian colonies sent contingents of
troops to South Africa to participate in the conflict. This is a history of the Tasmanian
contingent's contribution, written from the perspective of an Empire loyalist.

298   **A lion in the colony: an historical outline of the Tasmanian colonial voluntary military forces 1859-1901.**
D. M. Wyatt.   Hobart: The 6th Military District Museum, Anglesea Barracks, 1990. 62p. bibliog.

An historical outline of the formation, decline and subsequent redevelopment of the Tasmanian Voluntary Military Forces from their beginning in 1858 until the federation of the Australian colonies in 1901. Many historical photographs were uncovered during research and are included in the book. In 1987, Wyatt published a bigger work on the same subject but confined to the western part of Tasmania. It is *With the volunteers: a historical diary of the volunteer military forces of the north-west and west coasts of Tasmania 1886.* It contains hundreds of photographs depicting the life and activities of the volunteer soldier over the last 100 years.

Economics and Finance

299 Economic growth in Van Diemen's Land 1803-1821.
W. G. Rimmer.   In: *Economic growth of Australia 1788-1821.*
Edited by G. J. Abbott and N. B. Nairn.   Melbourne: Melbourne
University Press, 1969, p. 327-351.
This chapter should be read in conjunction with R. M. Hartwell's study *The economic development of Van Diemen's Land 1820-1850* (q.v.).

300 The economic development of Van Diemen's Land 1820-1850.
R. M. Hartwell.   Melbourne: Melbourne University Press, 1954. 273p.
bibliog.
A comprehensive account of the economic development of Tasmania from 1820, when, after sixteen years' occupation, the colony was still a tiny convict settlement of five and a half thousand people, to 1850, when the population had reached 70,000 and the colony had achieved a well-developed economy based on the produce of the land.

301 Foundations of the Australian monetary system 1788-1851.
S. J. Butlin.   Sydney: Sydney University Press, 1953. 727p. bibliog.
A history of Australian banks and banking and the development of the monetary system. There are many sections of the book dealing with Tasmanian banks and banking. A sequel to this work was published in 1986: *The Australian monetary system 1851 to 1914*; it was compiled after the author's death and edited by his daughter Judith F. Butlin from material left by her father. Both volumes contain abundant statistical material in several appendices.

302 The tariff in the Australian colonies 1856-1900.
G. D. Patterson.   Melbourne: Cheshire, 1968. 174p.
This is a historical survey of tariff policy showing the origins of import control and focusing on Victoria and New South Wales. Tasmania is treated separately in the chapters relating to the smaller colonies.

303 **Van Diemen's Land, 1811-26; Van Diemen's Land, 1826-51; Van Diemen's Land, 1851-1901.**
In: *Smugglers and sailors: the Customs history of Australia 1788-1901.*
David Day. Canberra: Australian Government Publishing Services,
1992, p. 128-141, 227-259.

In this definitive work of the six colonial Customs services in the nineteenth century,
three chapters are devoted to Tasmania. Being major revenue collectors for the colonial
governments, the Customs houses played an important role in colonial economic
life. Consequently, much can be learned from this book of the economic history of
Tasmania.

304 **Coins and tokens of Tasmania 1803-1910.**
Roger V. McNeice. Hobart: Platypus Publications, 1969. 112p.
bibliog.

The author is founder and past secretary of the Tasmanian Numismatic Society.
Although the main purpose of the book is to serve numismatists, it is also a history of
currency in Tasmania and contains much information on banks and banking and the
general development of the economy in the first hundred years.

305 **Launceston Bank for Savings 1835-1970: a history of Australia's
oldest savings bank.**
E. A. Beever. Melbourne: Melbourne University Press, 1972. 231p.
bibliog.

Because the Launceston Bank for Savings has operated as a regional institution from
the date of its establishment, its history is necessarily also the history of northern
Tasmania. In every aspect the Bank's activities have been closely interrelated with the
development of the region. On the occasion of its 150th anniversary in 1985 the Bank
published a pamphlet, edited by R. A. Ferrall, entitled *A proud heritage: the story of
the LBS Statewide Bank 1835-1985.*

306 **The Hobart Savings Bank: a review of its centenary of progress.**
Hobart Savings Bank, with a foreword by F. Leslie Langford,
President. Hobart: J. Walch & Sons, 1945. 78p.

An in-house publication to celebrate one hundred years of the Bank.

307 **In trust for 150 years.**
Jennifer Pringle-Jones. Hobart: Trust Bank, 1995. 126p.

While the Trust Bank is a young financial institution, established in 1991, its roots
date back a century and a half – to the early days of the colony of Van Diemen's Land.
Trust Bank is the result of the integration of two old Tasmanian community banks –
the SBT and Tasmania Banks – with a combined history of 300 years. This book is a
history of the Trust Bank and its forerunners, which have always been closely linked
with Tasmania's economic and social history.

Business and Industry

308 **Industrial awakening: a geography of Australian manufacturing 1788 to 1890.**
G. J. R. Linge.   Canberra: Australian National University Press, 1979. 845p. maps. bibliog.
Although in the main this scholarly work on the history of manufacturing industries in Australia relates to New South Wales and Victoria where the main development took place, there are two separate sections on Tasmanian developments: the first deals with the years 1815 to 1850, p. 118-135; the second covers the years from 1851 to 1890, p. 633-663. The reader is also referred to the index entries.

309 **Tasmanian inventions.**
Launceston: Queen Victoria Museum and Art Gallery, 1987. 60p. bibliog.
'A catalogue produced for an exhibition to document Tasmania's long tradition of innovation and ingenuity'. The four chapters of text present a history of inventions and innovations in Tasmania.

310 **Cascade: a taste of history.**
Mike Bingham.   Hobart: The Cascade Brewery Company, 1992. 216p. bibliog.
A history of the oldest brewery in Australia, the Cascade Brewery in Hobart, which has been slaking the thirst of Tasmanians since it was first established on its original site in 1824. The book is well produced and contains many historic illustrations.

311 **ENT: a corporate history.**
Brian Clark.   Launceston: A. W. Birchalls, 1994. 102p.
The story of a Tasmanian media company, by one of its long-time employees, which owned the Launceston *Examiner* (q.v.) and television interests before a successful takeover bid in 1994 led to its demise.

312   **Potlines and people: a history of the Bell Bay aluminium smelter.**
Brian Carroll.   Melbourne: Comalco Limited, 1980. 80p.

An account of the history of the aluminium industry at Bell Bay, on the Tamar River,
55 km from Launceston. The book also tells why Australia established an aluminium
industry and why Bell Bay was chosen as its site.

313   **The Zinc Works: producing zinc at Risdon 1916-1991.**
Alison Alexander.   Hobart: Pasminco Metals-EZ, 1992. 359p. bibliog.

The Zinc Works has been one of Tasmania's largest industrial undertakings since
1916. This is a detailed history of its development written from the point of view of
the thousands of men and women who worked there during a 75-year period. The
author, a trained historian, has also written a history of the Risdon Community
Council. It is entitled *A heritage of welfare and caring: the EZ Community Council
1918-1991* and was published in 1991. Both books are generously illustrated with
black-and-white photographs.

314   **I excell: the life and times of Sir Henry Jones.**
Bruce Brown.   Hobart: Libra Books, 1991. 207p. bibliog.

The life story of the Tasmanian industrial magnate Sir Henry Jones (1862-1926) who
rose from humble beginnings to controlling a vast network of business interests in
Australia and internationally. The book is more than a biography of a remarkable
businessman and his company H. Jones and Co. with its distinctive logo IXL; it is also
an important history of business and industry in Tasmania. Major business dynasties
either began or were associated with Jones. After Jones's death in 1926, the IXL
empire survived until 1972 when it finally succumbed to a take-over bid.

315   **The wind you say.**
Claudio Alcorso.   Sydney: Angus & Robertson, 1993. 170p.

The autobiography of Claudio Alcorso, who emigrated to Australia from Italy in 1937.
After internment during World War II, he became a successful businessman and patron
of the arts. Since 1947 he has lived in Tasmania and has established a pioneering
vineyard – Moorilla – in the Derwent Valley near Hobart. He was also involved in the
battle for the preservation of the Franklin River.

316   **Captain James Kelly of Hobart Town.**
K. M. Bowden.   Melbourne: Melbourne University Press, 1964. 126p.
maps. bibliog.

A scholarly life of James Kelly, one of the most adventurous of the early Hobart
whaling masters. Apart from becoming the master of a whaling and sealing fleet,
Kelly was at the centre of many colourful exploits, among the most outstanding of
these being the first circumnavigation of Tasmania in a whale-boat.

317 **'Big' Clarke.**
Michael Clarke.   Melbourne: Queensberry Hill Press, 1980. 284p.
bibliog.

William John Turner Clarke (1805-74), pastoralist and landowner, lived in Tasmania until 1850 and acquired large landholdings there as well as in Victoria and elsewhere. When he died in Victoria in 1874 he left an estate worth some £2.5 million, besides approximately 215,000 acres of freehold land throughout Australasia, a huge fortune by the standards of the times. This is a biography of 'Big' Clarke or 'Moneyed' Clarke as he was generally known, by a descendant.

318 **The luck of the draw: a centenary of Tattersall's sweeps 1881-1981.**
Trevor Wilson.   Melbourne: Wilson Publishing, 1980. 210p.

In the 1890s, at a time when the mainland colonies were legislating against the promotion of sweepstakes consultations, Tasmania accepted the most prominent sweepstake proprietor, George Adams and his Tattersall's organization, to operate in Tasmania. Tattersall's ran lotteries and sweepstakes consultations here until the mid-1950s, when operations were transferred to Victoria. Although the book has an Australia-wide focus, the Tasmanian gambling story features prominently.

319 **A million horses: Tasmania's power in the mountains.**
Compiled by R. M. H. Garvie.   Hobart: The Hydro-Electric Commission of Tasmania, 1962. 111p. maps. bibliog.

The statutory responsibility of the Hydro-Electric Commission of Tasmania is to generate, transmit, distribute and sell electricity. This is an in-house publication by the Commission about its heydays, well before the controversies and battles with conservationists in the 1970s and 1980s, which resulted, on the one hand, in the flooding of Lake Pedder, but on the other, in the abandonment of the Lower Gordon power development due to a High Court decision in 1983.

320 **Hydro Construction Villages.**
Sarah Rackman. Edited by Joan Woodberry.   Hobart: Public Relations Department, The Hydro-Electric Commission, 1981-83. 3 vols. maps. bibliogs.

The three volumes cover the history and the lifestyle of people living in the Tasmanian Hydro-Electric Commission's Construction Villages. The workers in these villages were employed in construction projects for the Commission. Volume I includes: Waddamana, Shannon and Tarraleah; volume 2: Butlers Gorge, Bronte Park, Trevallyn and Wayatinah; volume 3: Poatina, Gowrie Park and Strathgordon. Historic photographs illustrate all three volumes.

321 **Undermining Tasmania: a research paper on the mining industry.**
Bob Burton.   Hobart: Wilderness Society, 1989. 64p. maps. bibliogs.

A critical examination of the real benefits which Tasmanians receive from a non-renewable resource such as mining. The argument is pitched against traditionalist views which in Tasmania ignore the necessity to develop a sustainable economy.

322 **The Tasmanian forest industries.**
Elizabeth Hayward. Launceston: Tasmanian Timber Promotion
Board and the Forest Industries Association of Tasmania, 1990. 63p.

'This booklet has been jointly produced by the Tasmanian Timber Promotion Board and the Forest Industries Association of Tasmania to provide general information about the State's forest-based industries.'

323 **Sawing, selling & sons: histories of Australian timber firms.**
Edited by John Dargavel. Canberra: Centre for Resource and
Environmental Studies, Australian National University, 1988. 177p.
bibliogs.

Of the 31 chapters in the book several deal exclusively with the establishment of the timber industry in Tasmania and individual timber firms and sawmills in the island state.

324 **Australian Newsprint Mills Limited 1938-1988.**
Research and text by Rowan Burns. Hobart: ANM, 1988. 56p.

Australian Newsprint Mills Limited is Australia's only manufacturer of newsprint and the company has held this position since the start-up of the first paper machine at the Boyer Mill on 22 February 1941. The Boyer Mill has been the economic heart of the Derwent Valley near Hobart for 50 years. The book presents the story of this Tasmanian mill and that of the Albury Mill on the mainland which started production in 1981.

325 **Hearts of oak: the story of the southern forests.**
Bill Leitch. Huonville: Southern Holdings, 1990. 240p. map. bibliog.

Written by a man involved for many years in the timber industry, this is a history with some fictional characters, of the timber industry set in the exploitative or pioneering era of forestry in Tasmania. The book contains many period photographs.

326 **'A whitebait and a bloody scone . . .': an anecdotal history of APPM.**
Written and edited by Tess Lawrence. Melbourne: Jezebel Press,
1986. 68p.

This book was commissioned to mark the 50th anniversary of the founding of Associated Pulp and Paper Mills (APPM), a large part of whose operations are carried out in Tasmania, including the big paper mill at Wesley Vale near Devonport. The book presents the story of APPM mainly through the words and eyes of its employees at all levels, both past and present – it is an oral history of the company.

327 **Kauri 100 years: the centenary of Kauri Timber Company Limited 1888-1988.**
Kerry Pink. Smithton: Kauri Timber Company, 1988. 79p.

Floated in 1888 in Melbourne, Kauri Timber is one of Australia's biggest hardwood producers from its Chatlee complex near Smithton on Tasmania's north-west coast.

28   **Whaling ways of Hobart Town.**
     J. E. Philp.   Hobart: Walch, 1936. 95p.
Whaling was Tasmania's first primary industry. Starting from 1804, whaling
flourished for well over 100 years. This is a chatty account of the industry around
Hobart in the 20th century.

Agriculture and Pastoralism

329 **Memories of Myrtle Bank: the bush farming experiences of Rowland and Samuel Skemp in north-eastern Tasmania 1883-1948.**
John Rowland Skemp.   Melbourne: Melbourne University Press, 1952. 256p.

Although written around the early bush farming experiences of Rowland and Samuel Skemp at Myrtle Bank in north-eastern Tasmania, the book is much more than the story of a single pioneering undertaking. It is a vignette of history, giving a small but intensely detailed picture of both a district and an era. It portrays the folkways of the people of the area and records the growth of a community. It is a very readable book, written with humour and sensitivity.

330 **Tasmanian pastoral.**
Kathleen Graves.   Melbourne: Melbourne University Press, 1953. 143p. maps.

This book is based on 12 months of living and working on Woodlands, a property in the Mersey Valley near Deloraine, westwards of Launceston. The account is of the first year on the farm after the Graves family acquired ownership. It is an excellent representation of rural Tasmania at the time, written without pretension, yet with confidence, by an obviously cultured woman.

331 **We were the first.**
Seafield Deuchar.   Melbourne: Hawthorn Press, 1973. 53p.

Trowutta, a farming township at the edge of rainforest in the far north-west of Tasmania, was just being settled, when the author began farming there in the early 20th century. In this book of well-written prose he presents his pioneering experiences. The book includes reproductions in colour of some of Deuchar's many paintings. In his latter years he became an enthusiastic amateur painter of the local scenery.

332   **Full and plenty: an oral history of apple growing in the Huon Valley.**
Catherine Watson.   Hobart: Twelvetrees Publishing, 1987. 108p.
The Huon Valley, south of Hobart, is the centre of Tasmania's orchard industry. In these fascinating oral accounts, edited by the author, men and women who were intimately connected with the region remember their lives and recreate a way of living which predates sophisticated technology and the export consequences of Britain's entry into the Common Market.

333   **Old sheep for new pastures: a story of British sheep in the hands of Tasmanian colonial shepherds.**
Ivan C. Heazlewood.   Launceston: The Author, financed by the Tasmanian Branch of the Australian Society of Breeders of British Sheep, 1992. 257p. maps. bibliog.
A history of British sheep in Tasmania, from their early importation, their breeding, adapting them to local conditions, and their subsequent impact on Australian sheep in general. It is also, in effect, a history of the Tasmanian Branch of the Australian Society of Breeders of British Sheep. More broadly, the book also gives a general view of colonial and more recent rural life in Tasmania.

334   **Winton Merino Stud 1835-1985: a brief history of the Winton Merino Stud and the lives of the Taylor men who skillfully bred them for 150 years.**
Vera C. Taylor.   Geelong, Victoria: Neptune Press, 1985. 215p. maps. bibliog.
The Winton Merino Stud is believed to be the oldest existing and registered sheep stud in Australia and the labours of five generations of the Taylor family of Tasmania have contributed significantly to the improvement and maintenance of pure-bred Merinos, on which the Australian reputation for producting fine wool rests.

335   **Born of necessity: dairy co-operatives of Tasmania 1892-1992.**
Margery Godfrey, Ron Neilson.   Smithton: United Milk Tasmania Ltd, 1992. 232p.
A history of co-operative dairying in north Tasmania. The book was published to commemorate the centenary year of the first co-operative which is now the oldest member of United Milk Tasmania Ltd. This company comprises almost 500 farmer shareholders and more than 350 employees. With an annual turnover exceeding $100 million it contributes significantly to the Tasmanian economy.

336   **The dairy heritage of Northern Tasmania: a survey of the butter and cheese industry.**
Jill Cassidy.   Launceston: Queen Victoria Museum and Art Gallery, 1995. 243p. maps. bibliog.
Produced with funds provided by the Commonwealth Government under the National Estate Grants Program, this report presents a comprehensive history of the Tasmanian dairying industry.

337 **The hop industy in Australia.**
Helen R. Pearce.   Melbourne: Melbourne University Press, 1976.
263p. maps. bibliog.

Based on research undertaken for a Master of Arts thesis, this book is a detailed investigation of the development and history of the hop industry in Australia. Although small, the industry is important in a hot, beer-drinking country like Australia. As Tasmania has always been the premier hop-producing area, much of the book is concerned with the industry in the island state.

338 **Lifeblood of a colony: a history of irrigation in Tasmania.**
Margaret Mason-Cox.   Hobart: Rivers and Water Supply
Commission, 1994. 202p. maps. bibliog.

This book, commenced as an Australian bicentennial project, describes in detail many of the irrigation schemes put in place by the early white settlers of the colony of Van Diemen's Land. It fills a void in Tasmania's agricultural history.

339 **Midland Agricultural Association 1838-1988.**
Written and compiled by Vera C. Taylor, Patricia M. Taylor.
Campbell Town: Midland Agricultural Association, 1988. 148p.
bibliog.

The annual agricultural show is a feature of Australian life. Its primary function is to improve the standard of agriculture in the area in which it is held. Livestock and agricultural products are exhibited in competitive classes and prizes awarded by judges. In lightly populated areas the 'Show' is the highlight of the year. Held at Campbell Town, about 10 km south of Launceston, the Midland Agricultural Show is believed to be the oldest show in Australia. This book presents the story of 150 years of continuous shows. *Defying the odds: the history of the Burnie Agricultural and Pastoral Society*, by Annette Ebdon, gives an account of the Burnie Show.

340 **The Van Diemen's Land Company 1825-1842.**
A. L. Meston. Arranged for publication by W. M. Meston.
Launceston: Museum Committee Launceston City Council, 1958.
maps. bibliog. (Records of the Queen Victoria Museum Launceston.
New series, no. 9).

The Van Diemen's Land Company, a pastoral and agricultural organization, was founded by a London syndicate in 1825 to operate on land in northern Tasmania. In the same year the Colonial Office granted a block of land of about 100,000 hectares in the north-west of the island, Over time the Company has progressively sold off some of the land to encourage closer settlement. In 1988 it still held some 20,000 hectares and is continuing its pastoral activities with headquarters at Smithton on the north-west coast. This is a well-researched early history of the activities of the Company. An original employee of the Company, Jorgen Jorgenson, published a *History of the origin, rise and progress of the Van Diemen's Land Company* in 1829; it was reissued as a facsimile in 1979.

341 **Sketch of the history of Van Diemen's Land, illustrated by a map of the island, and an account of the Van Diemen's Land Company.**
James Bischoff.   Adelaide: Libraries Board of South Australia, 1967.
260p. map. (Australiana facsimile editions, no. 102).

The book was originally published in England in 1832 by the Company's Managing Director, resident in London, to inform the proprietors of the Van Diemen's Land Company about the colony in which they had invested. The larger portion of the book gives a history of the Company.

342 **Clyde Company papers.**
Edited by P. L. Brown.   London: Oxford University Press, 1941-71.
7 vols. maps. bibliogs.

The Scottish–Tasmanian syndicate known as the pastoral Clyde Company operated in Victoria for 23 years from 1836 to 1858, but its prosperity was based on 15 years of pastoral activities in Van Diemen's Land. The first three volumes spanning the years 1834 to 1845, are therefore of Tasmanian interest. The editor weaves together private papers with contemporary government records and colonial newspapers to give detailed information on the operations of the Company and the individuals associated with it. An earlier book (1935) *The narrative of George Russell of Golf Hill with Russellania and selected papers*, also edited by P. L. Brown, presents the experiences in Tasmania of George Russell who migrated from Scotland to Van Diemen's Land in 1831 and later became manager of the Company.

Transport and Communications

Communications

343 **A history of the Post Office in Tasmania.**
Compiled by the Australian Post Office in Tasmania. Hobart:
Australian Post Office, 1975. 72p.

An introductory history of postal services in Tasmania. Although the introduction states that the text has been compiled from both primary and secondary sources available in Tasmania, no bibliography is provided. There is also no index.

344 **Stamps and postal history of Tasmania.**
Walton Eugene Tinsley. London: The Royal Philatelic Society, 1986.
191p. bibliogs.

A wide-ranging coverage of Tasmanian philately for the beginner and general collector. The book also includes the history of postal services. A further good exposition of postal history and postal markings appears in a pair of volumes on the *Postal history and postal markings of Tasmania*, published by The Royal Philatelic Society of Victoria in 1967 and 1975. A. F. Basset Hull's *The stamps of Tasmania: a history of the postage stamps, envelopes, post cards . . .* (1890) is still useful. *The pictorial stamps of Tasmania 1899-1912*, by K. E. Lancaster, published in the J. R. W. Purvis Memorial Series by The Royal Philatelic Society of Victoria treats, at great length and in great detail, the series of stamps issued during 1899 and 1900, which were among the first pictorial stamps issued by a British colony.

345 **The semaphore telegraph system of Van Diemen's Land.**
W. E. Masters. Hobart: Cat & Fiddle Press, 1973. 46p. map.

Until the construction of the electric telegraph and telephone services in the latter half of the 19th century, the only means of telecommunication was by mechanical semaphores. This is a history of the semaphore as it operated in Tasmania.

346   **The story of the Bass Strait submarine telegraph cable 1859-1967.**
J. G. Branagan.   Launceston: Regal Publications, 1987. 44p.
When the Bass Strait cable was first installed to link Tasmania to the mainland, it was
he first underwater line in the southern hemisphere and the longest in the world. The
ast cable was laid in 1936 and taken out of service in 1967 when communication by
·adio was established.

Land transport

347   **Convicts and carriageways: Tasmanian road development until
1880.**
Lyn Newitt.   Hobart: Department of Main Roads, 1988. 332p. maps.
bibliog.
This large volume, richly illustrated with contemporary facsimiles of drawings, maps,
plans and textual extracts was published as a Tasmanian Bicentennial project. The
preface states the limitation on the scope of the work: 'The volume of suitable
material found created the need to limit the scope of the research to the period 1804-
1880, when a large proportion of the state's land transport transferred to the railways,
and mechanical methods were gradually introduced into the road building techniques
of the time.'

348   **Horse power.**
K. M. Dallas.   Devonport: Fuller's Bookshop, 1968. 100p.
Discusses the importance of horses in the development of Tasmania.

349   **A century of Tasmanian railways 1871-1971.**
Prepared for the Transport Commission Tasmania by H. J. W. Stokes.
Hobart: Government Printer, 1971. 31p. map.
A departmental publication giving a clear overview of the development of railways in
Tasmania. Although no sources are acknowledged, the booklet seems to be compiled
from departmental records. A privately published booklet to mark the centenary is
Railway centenary in Tasmania, by train buff William A. Bayley, who, while
providing some history, writes amusingly of the week-long Centenary Celebrations
from 7 to 14 February 1971.

350   **Railroading in Tasmania 1868-1961.**
Thomas C. J. Cooley.   Hobart: Government Printer, 1963.
157p. + 202 plates. maps.
An account of various Tasmanian government and private railways. Cooley is not the
sole author; some chapters are written by other people, including two chapters by
Professor W. A. Townsley. In his introduction Cooley writes that the book is not a
history but rather 'the story of the construction and running of both Government and
private railroads in Tasmania, together with stories of the trials and tribulations that

went with them . . .'. There are 202 illustrations, mainly of locomotives and rolling stock, stations and country traversed. Cooley published a similar work – *A history of trains and tramways in Tasmania* – in 1987. Both books suffer from not quoting sources. No index is provided either.

351 **Early steam in Tasmania: the first 17 years of 'broad gauge' railway in Tasmania – the struggle, the hardship and tragedy plus a 22-page feature on the tall ships that were involved.**
Brian Chamberlain. Launceston: Regal Press, 1987. 146p.

The preface states: 'The events recorded in this publication commenced just prior to the Launceston and Western Railway being registered as a company in 1867, continuing until its financial collapse during 1872 and on till the broad gauge era ended in 1888.'

352 **A history of railways and tramways on Tasmania's west coast.**
Lou Rae. Hobart: Mercury-Walch, 1984. 2nd ed. 212p. maps. bibliog.

A detailed account of the major railway and tramway systems which operated on the wild west coast of Tasmania from the beginning in the 19th century to the 1960s. Today, with the construction of better roads, the railway system has all but disappeared. The book is extensively illustrated with photographs, many of which have not been published previously. They provide a unique visual record of people, machines and landscape.

353 **The Emu Bay Railway: VDL Company to Pasminco.**
Lou Rae. Hobart: The Author, 1992[?]. 274p. map. bibliog.

A history of the Emu Bay Railway Company which was created to exploit the mineral wealth of the rich mining region on Tasmania's west coast. For approximately seventy years the Emu Bay Railway was essential to the region's mining industry.

354 **Hobart tramways: a centenary commemoration review.**
Ian G. Cooper. Sydney: Transit Australia, 1993. 65p. map. bibliog.

September 1993 marked the centenary of the commencement of the operation of electric trams in Hobart, the first successful electric tramway system in the southern hemisphere. The system ceased operating in 1960 when trams were replaced by buses. This book, illustrated with many black-and-white photographs of rolling stock, presents a history of the public transport service.

355 **Trolley buses of Tasmania.**
Ian G. Cooper. Sydney: Australian Electric Traction Association, 1980. 87p. maps. bibliog.

This is the story of the trolley bus services in Hobart and Launceston, where they were for many years the most important form of urban transport. With approximately 3 per cent of Australia's population, Tasmania operated 28 per cent of the country's trolley buses. Tasmania was the only state where two cities operated trolley bus systems. Many black-and-white photographs illustrate the text.

Shipping

356   **Guiding lights: Tasmania's lighthouses and lighthousemen.**
Kathleen M. Stanley.   Hobart: St David's Park Publishing, 1991.
181p.

A history of Tasmania's fourteen lighthouses, from the establishment of the first at
Iron Pot (at the entrance to the River Derwent) in 1832, to the present. The author is
the daughter of a lighthouse-keeper and spent much of her childhood on lighthouses.
As this is the first comprehensive record of Tasmania's lighthouses, it is a pity that the
author does not provide a bibliography and an index. There are numerous black-and-
white photographs.

357   **One hundred years, 1858-1958: the Marine Board of Hobart.**
Hobart: Marine Board of Hobart, 1958. unpaged.

The preface states: 'This brochure portrays, briefly, the development of the Port of
Hobart from the days of the first settlement by Governor Collins, and is published by
the Board in commemoration of the centenary of its establishment.'

358   **The story of the port of Launceston.**
R. A. Ferrall. With a preface by Captain Sir John Williams.
Launceston: Port of Launceston Authority, 1983. 136p.

This book was published to mark the 125th year of the Marine Board of Launceston,
later to be known as the Port of Launceston Authority.

359   **The quiet achievers: the history of the Port of Devonport.**
Maureen Bennett.   Launceston: Regal Press, 1995. 253p. bibliog.

The Port of Devonport has always played an important role in Tasmania's economic
development. The present book is an exhaustive, up-to-date documentation of the
Port's history and its contribution to the development of the north-west coast.
Although drawing heavily on the official records of the various authorities which have
been responsible for the Port during its existence, it also includes anecdotal evidence.
Today the Port is the terminal of the Bass Strait ferry service which connects
Tasmania to the mainland.

360   **Gateway to progress: centenary history of the Marine Board of
Burnie.**
Peter G. Mercer.   Burnie: Marine Board of Burnie, 1969. 206p.
bibliog.

Published to commemorate the centenary in 1968 of the Marine Board of Burnie, the
book necessarily also examines the agricultural, mining and industrial factors
responsible for the growth of the Port of Burnie. Thus it is also a history of Burnie and
north-west Tasmania.

361 **The shipping history of the Bass Strait crossing.**
Written and compiled by David Hopkins. Devonport: Taswegia, 1994. 37p. map.

Being an island, Tasmania, since European settlement, has been totally dependent on shipping and more recently also on air traffic, to overcome the watery barrier of Bass Strait, which separates it from mainland Australia. This profusely illustrated book chronicles some of the regular ships and ferries which transported passengers and cargo across the Strait.

362 **Ships in Tasmanian waters: riverboats, ferries and the floating bridge.**
G. W. Cox. Hobart: Fuller's Bookshop, 1971. 224p. maps.

This is an account of Tasmanian coastal and river steamers. Most of these small vessels plied their trade on the River Derwent where, in the days before roads were built, they were the only means of transport.

363 **Song of steam: a chronicle of paddle steamers and screw steamers in Tasmanian waters 1832-1939.**
D. G. O'May. Hobart: Government Printer, 1976. 304p.

Being an island, Tasmania was solely dependent on shipping for transport until the advent of aviation. During the first thirty years after the colony was founded, trade was carried on entirely by sailing ships. From 1832 steamships began to participate in the coastal and inter-colonial trade, and were followed a few years later by vessels from overseas. This book is not a complete account, but merely a record of some of the steamships, and in particular the pioneer steamers trading to and from Tasmania. There are many illustrations of the steamers discussed in the text.

364 **Pioneer shipping of Tasmania: whaling, sealing, piracy, shipwrecks, etc. in early Tasmania.**
L. Norman. Hobart: Shearwater Press, 1989. 220p.

The book was first published in 1938. It is a compendium of facts on Tasmania's maritime history, concentrating on ships and sea-related activities such as whaling and sealing. A companion volume by Norman entitled *Sea wolves and bandits: sealing, whaling, smuggling, and piracy, wild men of Van Diemen's Land, bushrangers and bandits, wrecks and wreckers* appeared in 1946. This book also contains a chronology of historical facts.

365 **Blue gum clippers and whale ships of Tasmania.**
Bill Lawson and the Shiplovers' Society of Tasmania. Melbourne: Georgian House, 1949. 261p.

Describes ships and shipbuilding in early Tasmania as well as whaling vessels and operations in Tasmanian waters. An appendix lists wrecks in Tasmanian waters and Tasmanian vessels until 1930. The index refers only to the ships mentioned in the text.

366 **Hobart river craft, and Sealers of Bass Strait.**
Compiled by Harry O'May. Hobart: Government Printer, 1959.
113 + 31p. map.

The author provides a chatty and anecdotal account of the early river trade which, in the absence of roads, served for communication and trade in the early days of the colony of Tasmania. *Sealers of Bass Strait* provides, in a similar vein, a short account of the sealing industry which lasted only till 1838 as, by that time, the seal population in Bass Strait had been so drastically reduced, that it was no longer profitable to catch them. O'May has also published *Wooden hookers of Hobart Town, and Whalers out of Van Diemen's Land*.

367 **Bass Strait ketches.**
Harold Salter. Hobart: St David's Park Publishing, 1991. 330p. maps.
bibliog.

An account of the small boats and ships which plied their trade in Bass Strait, linking the remote seaports of Tasmania, Victoria and South Australia. Often, these members of the 'mosquito fleet' were the main lifeline for many of the isolated coastal towns, settlements and farms, until land transport became sufficiently developed to replace them. The book is well illustrated with photographs and the author's own artwork, sketches and diagrams.

368 **The Tasmanian trading ketch: an illustrated oral history.**
Garry Kerr. Portland, Victoria: Mains'l Books, 1987. 179p. maps.

A history, based on transcripts of interviews with the men who built and sailed them, of Tasmanian wooden trading vessels during the first half of the 20th century, until the building of them ceased soon after World War II. The book contains 15 hull, sail and construction plans of differing types of Tasmanian-built trading vessels.

369 **The Tamar Boats: a complete reference book.**
Betty J. Percy. Launceston: Foot & Playsted, 1993. 260p. map. bibliog.

A chronological record of privately owned boats, built and launched on the Tamar River in northern Tasmania. All available details about each boat are given. There is an alphabetical index of the boats and many illustrations are included.

370 **Sail on the tide: the story of Flinders Island shipping 1953-1994.**
Leedham C. Walker. Hobart: The Author, 1994. 96p. map.

A history of the Flinders Strait Shipping Company, which provides the total shipping service for the island community. The author was Chairman of Directors of the company from 1960 to 1990.

371 **Wrecks in Tasmanian waters 1797-1950.**
Compiled by Harry O'May. Hobart: Government Printer, 1952[?].
209p. map.

A chronological listing of vessels wrecked in Tasmanian waters together with descriptions of the circumstances surrounding each disaster. There is a photographic section of the ships wrecked and an alphabetical index to ships mentioned in the text. There is no acknowledgement of the sources consulted in compiling the book.

372 **Shipwrecks of Tasmania's wild west coast.**
Graeme Broxam.   Hobart: Navarine Publishing, 1993. 471p. maps.
bibliog. (Roebuck Society Publication, no. 44).

The west coast of Tasmania is one the most isolated, wildest and most dangerous yet
most beautiful coastlines in the world, where the giant rollers of the southern Indian
Ocean, unhindered by land for thousands of kilometres, sweep in from the west.
Shipwrecks have been plentiful here. This is a model for all shipwreck books. It is
well researched and illustrated, explains the circumstances surrounding each disaster,
often quoting extensively from contemporary documents, testimony and personal
observations. It is also well indexed – ships, persons, organizations.

373 **Poor souls they perished: the *Cataraqui*, Australia's worst
shipwreck.**
Andrew Lemon, Marjorie Morgan.   Melbourne: Hargreen Publishing,
1986. 188p. maps. bibliog.

Traces the history of the *Cataraqui*, an emigrant ship, which went down on reefs off
King Island in Bass Strait in 1845 with the loss of 400 lives – only nine people
survived.

Labour and Employment

374 **Ways of working.**
Jim Marwood. Photographs by Jim Marwood and others.   Sydney: Kangaroo Press, 1986. 160p. maps. bibliog.
This is a photographic essay accompanied by text, created from interviews with over a hundred workers in six Tasmanian industries. The industries were chosen by the author for their historical and economic importance. The sites chosen were the EZ Mine at Rosebery, the Hydro-Electric Commission Township of Tarraleah, the Department of Main Roads in Hobart, the Australian National Railways Workshops at Launceston, the James Nelson Textile Mill at Launceston and the Waverley Woollen Mills in Launceston.

375 **The picket: Tasmanian mine workers defend their jobs.**
Renfrey Clarke.   Sydney: Pathfinder Press, 1984. 167p.
An account, sympathetic to the mine workers, of the six-week strike and picket by workers at EZ Industries Rosebery zinc-lead mine in western Tasmania during August and September 1983. Black-and-white photographs of strike activities illustrate the text.

376 **Politics in a union: the Hursey case.**
Tas. Bull.   Sydney: Alternative Publishing Co-operative, 1977. 134p.
Between 1956 and 1959 the Hursey case often made the front pages in the national newspapers. Frank Hursey and his son Dennis were waterside workers in Hobart who had a dispute with their union. When the Hurseys refused to pay a levy imposed by the union for the support of the Australian Labor Party during an election campaign, they were expelled from the union. They took their case to the courts and, eventually, the High Court of Australia, on appeal from a judgment of the Supreme Court of Tasmania, found that the Waterside Workers Federation of Australia did have the legal power to impose, by democratic vote, a political levy. The author was at the time a member and officer of the union in Hobart.

377 **Hope amidst hard times: working class organisation in Tasmania 1830-1850.**
Michael Quinlan.   Sydney: Industrial Relations Research Centre, University of New South Wales, 1986. 88p. bibliog. (Industrial Relations Research Centre, Monograph no. 13).

This is one of the few secondary sources on Tasmanian trade union history. It details material on early trade unions including an examination of strikes.

378 **Colonial servitude: indentured and assigned servants of the Van Diemen's Land Company 1825-41.**
Jennifer Duxbury.   Melbourne: Department of History, Monash University, 1989. 66p. map. bibliog. (Monash Publications in History, no. 4).

This study of colonial servitude, as experienced by the Van Diemen's Land Company, formed in 1825 in London to exploit the large tracts of pastoral land in the north-west of the colony, demonstrates the Company's failure to make a harsh and oppressive system of bondage productive in the economic and social climate of the colony.

379 **World of work, work in Tasmania: a guide to resource collections.**
Kim Pearce.   Melbourne: National Centre for Australian Studies and Solitude Press, Hobart, 1992. 99p.

Lists repositories in Tasmania which hold both archival and printed material related to the 'world of work'. The introduction contains 'a select list of secondary sources which anyone researching work in Tasmania should consult'. The author provides a critical commentary on the works listed.

Natural Resources

380 **Land systems of Tasmania.**
Various authors. Hobart: Department of Agriculture, Tasmania, 1978-89. 7 vols.
The volumes describe seven regions, covering the whole of Tasmania, which have been identified as areas of land with similar geology, topography, soils, vegetation and rainfall. The physical and biological resources of each region are described in great detail with the aid of many maps, tables and diagrams. This work should aid reearchers who need basic resource information. Extensive bibliographies are included in each volume.

381 **Tasman Peninsula: is history enough? Past, present and future use of the resources of Tasman Peninsula.**
Edited by S. J. Smith. Hobart: Royal Society of Tasmania, 1989. 156p. maps. bibliogs.
As the site of the penal settlement of Port Arthur, the Tasman Peninsula is of considerable historical significance. This, combined with the natural beauty and unusual geological features, make the peninsula Tasmania's foremost tourist attraction. The book includes the papers presented to the Tasman Peninsula Symposium conducted by the Royal Society of Tasmania at Port Arthur in November 1986. They discuss the peninsula's natural and cultural resources and the way the human population has used and is using the region.

382 **Landscape and man: the interaction between man and environment in Western Tasmania. The Proceedings of a Symposium organized by the Royal Society of Tasmania.**
Edited by N. R. Banks, J. B. Kirkpatrick. Hobart: Royal Society of Tasmania, 1977. 199p. bibliogs.
The papers presented at the Symposium discuss the physical, biological and social environment, resource utilization, the impact of man on the land, and finally the future

91

of the region. It is a region of spectacular wilderness areas and includes the Lower Gordon and Franklin Rivers. Some years after the Symposium the battles between the conservation movement and the established interests took place here over the construction of the Franklin Dam, which ended in the celebrated victory for the conservationists.

383   **The lake country of Tasmania: a symposium conducted by the Royal Society of Tasmania at Poatina, Tasmania, November 11-12, 1972.**
Edited by R. M. Banks.   Hobart: Royal Society of Tasmania, 1973.
199p. maps.

The papers presented at the Symposium describe the natural environment and human exploitation of the natural resources of the unique environment in the Tasmanian highlands. There are over 4000 lakes in 10,000 square kilometres on the Central Plateau, which was formed originally by an uplift of the land to an altitude of several hundred metres.

384   **Minerals and gemstones of Tasmania and their locations.**
Keith E. Lancaster.   Melbourne: Gemcraft Publications, 1980. 55p.
maps.

The purpose of this book is to provide both local residents and visitors with accurate information concerning the localities where both gemstones and mineral specimens are likely to be found in Tasmania. A similar booklet is G. J. O'Brien's *A guide to rockhunting in Tasmania*, published in 1978.

385   **The peaks of Lyell.**
Geoffrey Blainey.   Hobart: St David's Park Publishing, 1993.
5th updated ed. 370p.

A history of the Mount Lyell Mining and Railway Company Ltd which has been mining copper on the west coast of Tasmania for nearly 100 years. The book first appeared in 1954 and was considerably updated for the second and third editions. For the fifth edition two new chapters have been written, mainly about events over the last 25 years, when the mining field faced a series of crises. Professor Blainey is the prolific author of many well-regarded works on Australian history. An excellent visual accompaniment to Blainey's book is Lou Rae's *The Mt Lyell Mining and Railway Co Ltd: a pictorial history 1893*-1993, published in 1993.

386   **A window on Rosebery: a pictorial review of the 100 years in and around the environs of Rosebery on Tasmania's rugged west coast 1893-1993.**
Lou Rae.   Ulverstone: Lou Rae, 1994. 94p.

Since 1893 Rosebery has been a settlement for the mining of silver-lead-zinc ores. This is a centenary history with many contemporary photographs.

387 **100 years of western Tasmanian mining.**
Kerry Pink. Zeehan: West Coast Pioneers' Memorial Museum, 1975.
59p.

A reproduction of a feature in the Burnie *Advocate* to commemorate the centenary of the discovery of tin at Mt Bischoff by 'Philosopher' Smith in 1871. The book describes the early mining days of Mounts Bischoff, Lyell and Read, and developments at Renison Bell, Savage River and Cleveland after World War II.

388 **The Port Arthur coal mines, 1833-1877.**
Ian Brand. Launceston: Regal Publications, 1993. 90p.

The story of the Plunkett Point mine, the first successful coal mine in Van Diemen's Land. It was begun by the authorities at the penal settlement of Port Arthur and worked by convicts until 1848 when the mine passed into private hands.

389 **Tasmania.**
In: *A history of forestry in Australia*. L. T. Carron. Canberra:
Australian National University Press, 1985, p. 59-94. bibliog.

An outline of the historical development of forestry in Tasmania from its beginnings to the present, with an emphasis on policy and administration, rather than on scientific and technological development.

390 **The eucalypti hardwood timbers of Tasmania and the Tasmanian ornamental and softwood timbers: a descriptive treatise on their commercial uses, with reports on their durability.**
Written and compiled by D. W. Lewin. Hobart: Gray Brothers, 1906.
140p.

Discusses the timber resources of Tasmania with some reference to the timber industry. An interesting publication for its time as it displays a historical perspective and expresses conservationist and aesthetic sentiments.

Environment

391 Tasmania's heritage: an enduring legacy.
Jennifer Pringle-Jones, Ray Joyce.   Hobart: St David's Park
Publishing, 1991. 144p.

About 20 per cent of Tasmania's 68,000 square-kilometre area has been included in
UNESCO's World Heritage List. In addition, Tasmania has more than 1300 places on
Australia's Register of the National Estate. The text and coloured photographs of this
large-format volume combine to present some of this rich heritage to the reader.
Landscape, flora, fauna, buildings, monuments, ruins and other structures are covered
by the book.

392 The rest of the world is watching: Tasmania and the Greens.
Edited by Cassandra Pybus, Richard Flanagan.   Sydney: Pan
Macmillan, 1990. 271p.

A series of essays by leading conservationists and experts in environmental politics
dealing with the origins and development of the Green movement in Tasmania. It
began with the campaign to save Lake Pedder from flooding in the late 1960s and
early 1970s which ended in failure, followed by other successful battles, notably the
famous Franklin River blockade.

393 A time to care: Tasmania's endangered wilderness.
Text by Norm Sanders. Photographs by Chris Bell. Foreword by Bob
Brown.   Blackmans Bay, Tasmania: Chris Bell, 1980. 112p. map.

An impassioned plea in words and pictures for the preservation of the beautiful
wilderness area in south-west Tasmania which is being exploited by dam builders,
loggers and miners.

394 **Our disappearing heritage: the cultural landscape of the Central Plateau.**

Simon Cubit, Des Murray.   Launceston: Regal Publications, 1993. 54p.

The latest of three books in which Cubit, whose family association with the region stretches back for generations, examines the relationship between human habitation and the environment in the central highlands of Tasmania. The other two books are *Snarers and cattlemen of the Mersey high country: the Lees of Lees Paddocks* (1987) and *A high country heritage* (1988). The latter two are illustrated with drawings by Des Murray.

395 **The south west book: a Tasmanian wilderness.**

Edited by Helen Gee, Janet Fenton.   Sydney: Collins and the Australian Conservation Foundation, 1983. 308p. maps. bibliog.

This big book is a mine of information about the south-west corner of Australia's smallest state. Assembled by various people with individual viewpoints it is a compendium about the people of the region, its geology and geography, its flora and fauna, and the threats of destruction posed by forestry, hydro-electric development, mining and tourism. The volume is well illustrated with photographs, maps, prints, sketches, diagrams and old newspaper cuttings. It is completed by an extended bibliography.

396 **South west Tasmania: a land of the wild.**

David Neilson.   Adelaide: Rigby, 1975. 176p. maps. bibliog.

A book of artistic photographs demonstrating the beauty of the natural environment of the region. The accompanying text has strong conservationist undertones.

397 **Beyond the reach: Cradle Mountain–Lake St Clair National Park.**

Chris Bell.   Hobart: Laurel Press, 1990. 95p.

Cradle Mountain–Lake St Clair National Park, established in 1922, is one of Tasmania's oldest parks. It is one of Australia's outstanding wilderness areas and contains some of the best mountain scenery in the country. Art photography of the natural environment is the focus of this book although there are short chapters on geology, natural history, and a plea for the conservation of the remaining wild areas in western Tasmania. A similar illustrated book, but also containing the history of the Park, is *Cradle country: a Tasmanian wilderness* by Mike McKelvey, published in 1976.

398 **A man and a mountain: the story of Gustav Weindorfer.**

Margaret Giordano.   Launceston: Regal Publications, 1987. 123p. maps. bibliog.

The story of pioneer conservationist Gustav Weindorfer, who arrived in Australia from his native Austria in 1900. After settling in Tasmania he battled for the rest of his life to fulfill a dream – the establishment of the Cradle Mountain–Lake Clair National Park. In 1922 success was achieved when a Scenic Reserve and Wildlife Sanctuary of 158,000 acres was proclaimed. In December 1982 it was added to the World Heritage List. An earlier book on Weindorfer based on extensive research is Dr G. F. J. Bergman's *Gustav Weindorfer of Cradle Mountain*, published in 1959. Many contemporary photographs enhance both books.

399 **The world of Olegas Truchanas.**
Max Angus.   Melbourne: Australian Conservation Foundation, 1980.
144p. maps. bibliog.

This book commemorates an outstanding pioneer of conservation in Tasmania. It consists mainly of evocative colour photographs taken by Truchanas during his extensive travels by canoe and on foot to the spectacular wilderness areas of the island. Accompanying the pictures is a memoir by Max Angus outlining Truchanas's life and his many achievements.

400 **Frederick Smithies O.B.E., explorer, mountaineer, photographer: a great Tasmanian.**
J. G. Branagan.   Launceston: Regal Press, 1985. 138p. maps. bibliog.

Fred Smithies was a pioneer environmentalist. He hiked and climbed in wilderness areas in the 1920s and 1930s and popularized them through illustrated lectures, at a time when awareness about the need for nature conservation was very limited.

401 **Power in Tasmania.**
Peter Thompson.   Melbourne: Australian Conservation Foundation, 1981. 192p. bibliog.

A former Australian Broadcasting Corporation current affairs journalist documents the complexities of the Tasmanian community's relationship with the Hydro-Electric Commission (HEC), which has dominated the State's political, industrial and economic policies for the greater part of this century. Only since the flooding of Lake Pedder in the early 1970s has the HEC become the centre of a heated debate about its undemocratic, behind-the-scenes influence on power development in Tasmania. For a contrasting, optimistic view of the HEC the reader may consult Peter Read's *The organization of electricity supply in Tasmania* published in 1986 by the University of Tasmania.

402 **Damania: the Hydro-Electric Commission, the environment and government in Tasmania.**
Edited by Richard Jones.   Hobart: Fuller's Bookshop, 1972. 112p.

These are the printed proceedings of a symposium sponsored by the Lake Pedder Action Committee, the Tasmanian Conservation Trust and the Australian Conservation Foundation. The symposium was held because conservationists were concerned about the Tasmanian government's neglect of environmental issues.

403 **Lake Pedder: why a national park must be saved.**
Writen and edited by Dick Johnson. Illustrated by John Brownlie.
Melbourne: Lake Pedder Action Committees of Victoria and Tasmania and the Australian Union of Students, 1972. 96p. maps. bibliog.

A publication by the conservationist forces opposed to the flooding of Lake Pedder by hydro-electric development.

404 **Lake Pedder.**
Bob Brown and others.   Hobart: The Wilderness Society, 1985.
Various pagings. maps.

Lake Pedder was the centre of a unique wilderness area in remote south-west Tasmania. In 1972, after a long struggle between conservationists and the Tasmanian government and the powerful Hydro-Electric Commission, the lake and its environs were obliterated by the Middle Gordon hydro-electric scheme. This book celebrates and perpetuates in photographs the memory of Lake Pedder. A short text describes the history of the area and the development of the events which led to its inundation.

405 **The fight for the Franklin: the story of Australia's last wild river.**
Bob Connolly.   Sydney: Cassell, 1981. 143p. maps.

In the summer of 1980 Bob Connolly and Robin Anderson rafted down the Franklin River to make a film for the Tasmanian Film Corporation. This is the story of their dangerous journey. It is also a study of the energy alternatives available to Tasmania and the author questions the economic viability of hydro-electricity. They returned from their journey convinced that conservationist moves to preserve the wilderness area of the Frankin were justified and they joined the fight to preserve the river. The conservationists achieved a significant victory in 1983 when the High Court of Australia declared the dam construction illegal. Many evocative photographs accompany the text.

406 **Wild rivers: Franklin, Denison, Gordon.**
Photographs by Peter Dombrovskis. Text by Bob Brown.   Hobart:
Peter Dombrovskis Pty Ltd, 1983. 128p.

Wild rivers was published in the last months of the campaign to save Tasmania's wild rivers from the construction of the Gordon-below-Franklin dam. The book consists of vivid photographs of river scenery by professional photographer Dombrovskis, and the story of a journey by raft down the Franklin River by Bob Brown. Brown played a leading role in the conservationists' battle against the dam.

407 **The Franklin: not just a river.**
James McQueen.   Melbourne: Penguin Books, 1983. 83p. maps.

The well-known novelist tells the factual story of the struggle to save the Franklin River from destruction. He traces the formation and evolution of the conservation movement and portrays its leading personalities. He himself took part in the blockade of the Franklin River.

408 **Battle for the Franklin: conversations with the combatants in the struggle for south west Tasmania.**
Interviews by Roger Green. Photographs by Geoffrey Lea.   Sydney:
Fontana/Australian Conservation Foundation, 1981. 303p.

A series of interviews with the main participants, from both sides, including politicians, workers and conservationists in the battle to preserve the Franklin River from hydro-electric development and destruction. Green links the interviews with an introduction and commentaries throughout the book.

Environment

409   **The Franklin blockade.**
The blockaders.   Hobart: Wilderness Society, 1983. 123p.
A dramatic presentation in photographs and stories by those who took part in the
battle to save the Franklin River from being dammed by the authorities.

410   **Bob Brown of the Franklin River.**
Peter Thompson.   Sydney: Allen & Unwin, 1984. 203p. bibliog.
Journalist and fellow conservationist Peter Thompson tells the story of Dr Bob Brown
who achieved fame for his spirited defence of Tasmania's magnificent wilderness
areas. He was one of the leading participants in the struggle to preserve the Franklin
River in south-west Tasmania.

411   **The struggle for south-west Tasmania.**
Bruce Davis.   In: *Interest groups and public policy.*   Roger Scott.
Melbourne: Macmillan, 1980, p. 152-169.
A scholarly examination of the battle for the wilderness areas in south-west Tasmania
before the situation was resolved by the High Court of Australia in 1983.

412   **The Gordon and Franklin Rivers controversy: a bibliography.**
Compiled by Walter J. Lawson.   Brisbane: Griffith University
Library, 1986. 108p.
A list of references which is indispensable to anyone wanting to study the battle for
the preservation of the Gordon and Franklin Rivers from inundation. Newspaper and
periodical literature as well as government publications are useful inclusions in the
bibliography.

413   **The environmental effects of Mount Lyell operations on
Macquarie Harbour and Strahan.**
Alexandra D. De Blas.   Sydney: Australian Centre for Independent
Journalism, University of Technology, Sydney, 1994. 133p. maps.
bibliog.
This University of Tasmania thesis concerns possible environmental effects of the
Mount Lyell Mining and Railway Company's operations in Tasmania's Macquarie
Harbour and the community of Strahan. It has now been published, 18 months after
completion, following strenuous legal attempts by the Company to stop its release.
Appendix 5 presents a summary of press coverage relating to Mount Lyell's attempts
to suppress publication of the thesis.

Education

414 Making more adequate provision: state education in Tasmania, 1839-1985.
Derek Phillips. Research by Michael Sprod.   Hobart: A. B. Candell, Tasmanian Government Printer for the Education Department of Tasmania, 1985. 394p. bibliog.

This is the only general history of state education in Tasmania; Clifford Reeve's *History of Tasmanian education* (1935) dealt only with primary education. Phillips's book is concerned with the development of primary, secondary and technical education from their beginnings to the present. There are many black-and-white illustrations and an extensive bibliography guides to further reading.

415 An affirming flame: adventures in continuing education.
Kenneth G. Brooks.   Hobart: William Legrand Publishing, 1987. 208p.

This history of adult education in Tasmania has been written by an ex-Director of Adult Education from 1954 to 1968. It is based on the personal recollections of the author and those of his colleagues and associates, as well as archival records.

416 State aid and Tasmanian politics 1868-1920.
Richard P. Davis.   Hobart: University of Tasmania, 1980. 2nd ed. 87p.

First published in 1969, this second edition retains virtually the same text, with some updating. A second volume by Davis, an academic at the University of Tasmania, entitled *A guide to the state aid tangle in Tasmania* and published in 1974, takes the story of the controversial topic of state aid to Church schools from 1920 to 1974.

417   **With zealous efficiency: progressivism and Tasmanian state primary education 1900-20.**
G. W. Rodwell.   Darwin: William Michael Press, 1992. 279p. bibliog.
The book is adapted from a PhD thesis and suffers in some ways from the transition. Nevertheless it provides a valuable examination of the major theoretical influences on Tasmania's system of primary education as it operated until well after World War II.

418   **A tale of two cities: Mechanics' Institutes in Hobart and Launceston.**
Stefan Petrow.   In: *Pioneering culture: Mechanics' Institutes and Schools of Arts in Australia.*   Edited by P. C. Candy, John Laurent. Adelaide: Auslib Press, 1994, p. 311-326.
The Mechanics' Institutes and Schools of Art were vital community centres in the 19th century – the forerunners not only of municipal libraries, but also of many technical colleges and adult education centres. Dr Petrow here presents the history of two of the most influential Institutes in Tasmania. An extensive bibliography accompanies the chapter.

419   **Thomas Arnold the Younger in Van Diemen's Land.**
P. A. Howell.   Hobart: Tasmanian Historical Research Association, 1964. 60p. bibliog.
Thomas Arnold the Younger, son of Arnold of Rugby, was Inspector of Schools and Secretary to the Board of Education in Van Diemen's Land from 1850 until his return to England in 1856. The book examines his contribution to the development of the public education system in the colony.

420   **Open to talent: the centenary history of the University of Tasmania 1890-1990.**
Richard Davis.   Hobart: University of Tasmania, 1990. 256p. bibliog.
A detailed history of the University of Tasmania, the fourth oldest in Australia, by a professor of history at the institution. The text is accompanied by many black-and-white photographs.

421   **Edmund Morris Miller 1881-1964.**
In: *Nine Australian progressives: vitalism in bourgeois social thought 1890-1960.*   Michael Roe.   Brisbane: University of Queensland Press, 1984, p. 280-314.
A study of the life and scholarly career of E. Morris Miller, who was involved with the University of Tasmania from 1913, when he was appointed to a lectureship in philosophy and economics, through a term as vice-chancellor, to his retirement in 1951. All through his university career he was also actively involved in Tasmania's public life.

422   **Gross moral turpitude: the Orr case reconsidered.**
Cassandra Pybus.   Melbourne: Heinemann, 1993. 238p. bibliog.
A re-examination of a *cause célèbre* in Hobart during the 1950s concerning
philosophy professor Sydney Sparkes Orr whose conflict with the University of
Tasmania over his suggested reforms of the composition of the University Council and
allegations about his sexual misconduct eventually led to his dismissal from his post.
An earlier book, W. H. C. Eddy's *Orr*, published in 1961, is a detailed and passionate
764-page defence of the professor.

423   **The history of the Australian Maritime College.**
Alison Alexander, assisted by a Committee consisting of Barrie
Lewarn (Chair) and others.   Launceston: Australian Maritime
College, 1994. 196p. bibliog.
Established in 1980 in Launceston, the Australian Maritime College is Australia's first
and only specialist maritime studies institution. It offers courses in shipping, fishing
technology, electronics, engineering and maritime business. This is a history of the
College, including events leading up to its establishment.

424   **A place for art: a century of art, craft, design and industrial arts
education in Hobart.**
Created by Lindsay Broughton, George Burrows and Elizabeth Lada.
Project Co-ordinator: George Burrows.   Hobart: University of
Tasmania, in conjunction with the Hobart Technical College, 1988.
96p. bibliog.
The exhibition *A place for art*, held at the University of Tasmania from September to
October 1988, marked the centenary year of the Hobart Technical College. It
presented a survey of 104 years of art, craft and design education in Hobart from 1884
to the present, through the agency of artworks, craft objects, photographs, old
equipment and other historical artefacts. While covering the same overall ground, the
essays included in this catalogue place a heavy emphasis on the period 1880 to 1920,
when crucial issues in art education were debated and settled.

425   **'The cultured mind – the skilful hand': a centenary history of the
Hobart Technical College.**
Jill Waters.   Hobart: Hobart Technical College, 1988. 247p. bibliog.
The book describes the development, from its establishment in 1888, of Hobart
Technical College and provides a record of the personalities involved in that develop-
ment. On a broader scale it also touches upon the significant development in technical
and further education in Tasmania at various times in the last one hundred years.

426   **Tasmanian Conservatorium of Music: beginning the journey – the
first 25 years.**
Lyndal Edmiston, Leon Stemler.   Hobart: The Authors, 1990. 54p.
Written for the 25th anniversary of the establishment of the Tasmanian Conservatorium of Music, the first music school in Tasmania.

427 The Allport Library and Museum of Fine Arts.

Hobart: State Library of Tasmania, 1993. Rev. ed. 32p.

This descriptive handbook, issued by the State Library, highlights the treasures of the Allport family collection of books and art, which the Library acquired in 1966.

428 The Hutchins School: Macquarie Street years 1846-1965.

Geoffrey Stephens.   Hobart: The Hutchins School, 1979. 408p. bibliog.

A scholarly history of one of the oldest Church schools in Australia. It was written by the school's chaplain for the occasion when the school relocated to its new site in the Hobart inner suburb of Sandy Bay.

429 The story of the Launceston Church Grammar School.

Basil W. Rait. Appendices by Bernard Gordon.   Launceston: The School Centenary Committee, 1946. 200p.

A centenary history of one of the great public schools in Australia, a sister establishment of the famous Hutchins School in Hobart. In this book much can also be learnt of the development of Church of England education in Tasmania in general. The appendices are devoted to many activities in the school in the form of detailed and tabulated summaries. The equivalent girls' school in Launceston is the Church of England Girls' Grammar School and its story is told by Faith Layton in *An establishment for young ladies: Broadland House*, published in 1991.

430 The rose and the waratah: the Friends' School Hobart, formation and development 1832-1945.

William Nicolle Oats.   Hobart: The Friends' School, 1979. 304p. bibliog.

The story of Quaker education in Tasmania up to 1945, when the author became the Friends' School's headmaster. He relinquished the post in 1973. Oats brings a wealth of experience as well as scholarship to the writing of this story. A more traditional school history was published by the School in 1961 – *The Friends' School 1887-1961: the seventy-fifth anniversary*. This contains pictures and names of both pupils and teachers and governors and also provides a chronological account of the School's development.

Literature and Language

General and critical

431 **Tasmanian literary landmarks.**
Margaret Giordano, Don Norman.   Hobart: Shearwater Press, 1984.
202p.
Tasmania can claim some important firsts in Australian literary development: the first novelist, Henry Savery; the first playwright, David Burn; the first dramatic critic, early short-story writer and essayist, Thomas Richards; and the first published novel about the convict system, Caroline Leakey's *The broad arrow*. *Tasmanian literary landmarks* presents a non-academic account of the lives of 29 creative writers and the places most associated with them in Tasmania. Photographs complement the text.

432 **Tasmania.**
In: *The Oxford literary guide to Australia.*   General editor Peter Pierce, for the Association for the Study of Australian Literature.
Melbourne: Oxford University Press, 1993. Rev. ed., p. 239-285.
The first literary guide to Australia is now published in a fully revised paperback edition. The introduction states: 'This book is a celebration of Australian literary landscapes. It is a record of the many responses writers have made to the natural and constructed sites of the continent. Entries include towns, townships, suburbs, rivers, mountains and well-known geographical areas . . . and appear alphabetically . . . The grounds for inclusion are the biographical and imaginative associations which authors have formed with these places. They represent sites from which the writers drew their inspiration; sites where writers have lived and worked and drunk, have been educated, have married, have died and are buried.'

433 **Pressmen and governors: Australian editors and writers in early Tasmania: a contribution to the history of the Australian press and literature with notes biographical and bibliographical.**
E. Morris Miller.   Sydney: Sydney University Press, 1973. 308p. bibliogs.

An investigation into journalism and the bitter struggle for the independence of the press in early Van Diemen's Land. This is a facsimile edition of the book first published in 1952.

434 **Countries of the mind: the biographical journey of Edmund Morris Miller (1881-1964).**
John Reynolds, Margaret Giordano.   Hobart: Melanie Publications, 1985. 172p. bibliog.

The biography of a man active in the cultural life of Tasmania. He was vice-chancellor of the University of Tasmania from 1933 to 1945 and the compiler of the landmark work, the two-volume bibliography, *Australian literature: from its beginnings to 1935*. His research into early Tasmanian literature resulted in the publication of *Pressmen and governors: Australian editors and writers in early Tasmania* in 1952 (see item no. 433).

435 **Gwen Harwood: the real and imagined world.**
Alison Hoddinott.   Sydney: Angus & Robertson, 1991. 234p. bibliog.

A critical analysis of the work of Gwen Harwood, Tasmania's most famous poet, by a close friend of 40 years.

436 **A mortal flame. Marie Bjelke-Petersen: Australian romance writer 1874-1969.**
Alison Alexander.   Hobart: Blubber Head Press, 1994. 276p. bibliog.

Marie Bjelke-Petersen was a highly successful romantic novelist of her day. Her nine books, largely set in Tasmania, where she resided, were published between 1917 and 1937 and achieved total sales of 250,000 copies. This book is a very readable account of Bjelke-Petersen who for a woman of her time led a very unorthodox life.

437 **Doherty's Corner: the life and work of poet Marie E. J. Pitt.**
Colleen Burke.   Sydney: Sirius Books, 1985. 154p. bibliog.

Poet Marie E. J. Pitt spent the 1890s and early 1900s as a wife and mother in isolated mining camps on Tasmania's west coast. It was here she wrote her best poems which evoked the brooding melancholy of the west Tasmanian landscape. She was also a convinced socialist, active in politics, and this labourist attitude is expressed in the poems.

438   **Tassie terms: a glossary of Tasmanian words.**
Compiled by Maureen Brooks and Joan Ritchie at the Australian
National Dictionary Centre.   Melbourne: Oxford University Press,
1995. 174p. bibliog.

The book has resulted from a research programme into regional English in Australia at
the Australian National Dictionary Centre in Canberra. The words in *Tassie terms* are
not all exclusively Tasmanian, but collectively reflect the identity and spirit of the
island state. For example, Tasmanians, protected against their cold and rain by their
blueys (heavy, blue-grey coats) and blunnies (sturdy Blundstone boots), have enjoyed
or endured a long list of nicknames, including mutton birders (if they live in
Launceston), coutas or baracoutas (if in Hobart), Taswegians, Vandemonians,
Tasmaniacs and apple chewers. They call their state Tassie.

Fiction

439   **Storyline: short fiction by Tasmanian writers.**
Edited by Joan Birchall, Geoffrey Dean, Margaret Giordano.   Hobart:
Fellowship of Australian Writers (Tasmania), 1990. 136p.

An anthology of short stories by 23 Tasmanian writers. There is an appendix containing biographical notes on the authors. In 1979 the Fellowship published an earlier
collection: *An anthology of short stories, articles and poems by Tasmanian authors*,
edited by Joan Woodberry.

440   **Death of a river guide.**
Richard Flanagan.   Melbourne: McPhee Gribble, 1994. 326p.

A novel which treats important Tasmanian issues of recent years: the fate of
Tasmania's Aborigines, the island's terrible history as a penal colony and the relationship between the old Anglo-Celtic Australians and the children or descendants of
more recent immigrants from other parts of the world.

441   **The bluebird café.**
Carmel Bird.   Melbourne: McPhee Gribble, 1990. 180p.

A fascinating novel about the state of modern-day Tasmania and the way the present
has been shaped by its dark past.

442   **The boys in the island.**
Christopher Koch.   London: Hamish Hamilton, 1958. 250p.

A second version of this novel set in Tasmania appeared in 1974. Koch's second
Tasmanian novel appeared in 1985 – *The doubleman*. Both deal with the author's
perceived stifling social environment of Tasmania.

443 Hook's mountain.

James McQueen.   Melbourne: Sun Books, 1983. 214p.

This novel set in present-day rural Tasmania, its bush and vistas lovingly recreated by the author, is concerned with the meaning of violence in the context of a conservation battle.

444 I will not say the day is done.

Hesba Brinsmead-Hungerford.   Sydney: Alternative Publishing Cooperative, 1983. 164p.

A fictional account of the fight to save Lake Pedder from inundation, by a noted writer of children's books.

445 Doctor Wooreddy's prescription for enduring the ending of the world.

Colin Johnson.   Melbourne: Hyland House, 1983. 207p.

A novel by a well-known Aboriginal author, who also writes under the names of Mudrooroo Narogin and Mudrooroo, about the fate of the Tasmanian Aborigines. His *Master of the ghost dreaming* treats the same subject.

446 The savage crows.

Robert Drewe.   Sydney: Collins, 1976. 264p.

This first novel, by a highly successful Australian writer, deals with the fate of the Tasmanian Aborigines.

447 The morality of gentlemen.

Amanda Lohrey.   Sydney: Alternative Publishing Cooperative, 1984. 243p.

A novel about politics in Tasmania, based on a real-life waterside dispute in Hobart.

448 Drift.

Brian Castro.   Melbourne: Heinemann, 1994. 266p.

A complex novel about encounters between Aborigines and Europeans in early Tasmania which resulted in the genocide of the full-blood Tasmanian Aborigines.

449 For the term of his natural life.

Marcus Clarke. Introduced by Laurie Hergenhan.   Sydney: Angus & Robertson, 1992. 445p.

First published in book form in 1874, this classic novel of life in the penal colony of Tasmania has been widely translated and filmed several times. In this edition, it is reprinted with a new introduction.

450   **The bitter bread of banishment formerly** *Quintus Servinton*: **a tale**
      founded upon incidents of real occurrence.
      Henry Savery. Edited with a biographical introduction by Cecil
      Hadgraft. Sydney: New South Wales University Press, 1984. 392p.
      bibliog.

Henry Savery was transported for forgery and arrived in Hobart in 1825. He contributed articles to the local newspaper, a collection of which were published as the
first volume of Australian essays in 1830. His *Quintus Servinton* was the first
Australian novel published in Hobart in 1831. The novel provides the reader with an
authentic picture of convict life as seen through the eyes of an educated rogue.

451   **The tilted cross.**
      Hal Porter. London: Faber and Faber, 1961. 266p.

Set in Hobart in the 1840s this is a shocking and vivid novel about convict life in
Tasmania.

452   **Vandemon's daughter.**
      Joan Goodrick.   Adelaide: Rigby, 1974. 267p.

An historical novel set in the 1840s in the New Norfolk district of Tasmania. It is a
good rendition of colonial life.

Poetry

453   **Tasmania and Australian poetry.**
      Vivian Smith.   Hobart: University of Tasmania, 1984. 20p.
      (University of Tasmania. Occasional Paper, no. 37).

This is the text of the 1983 James McAuley Memorial Lecture delivered by Dr V. B.
Smith, Reader in English, University of Sydney, on 13 September 1983. Dr Smith is
himself a published poet.

454   **Effects of light: the poetry of Tasmania.**
      Edited by Vivian Smith, Margaret Scott.   Hobart: Twelvetrees
      Publishing Company, 1985. 175p.

In this anthology the editors have set themselves the task: 'to represent the best works
of poets born in Tasmania and of those from other parts of the world who have settled
at least temporarily in the island.' Also included are: 'a number of poems which
illustrate impressions that Tasmania and its surrounding oceans and archipelagos have
made upon poets who have encountered these places only in brief visits or at second
hand.' There is a general introduction, and biographical notes on the poets represented
in the volume.

455   Tide country.
Vivian Smith.   Sydney: Angus & Roberson, 1982. 93p.

Vivian Smith is a native-born Tasmanian poet, whose poems explore every aspect of the Tasmanian landscape.

456   Remote corners.
Graeme Hetherington.   Hobart: Twelvetrees Publishing Company, 1986. 41p.

The author of this collection of poetry grew up in the remote west coast mining towns of Tasmania. Set mostly in a rural environment, these poems evoke a powerful sense of place, inhabited by miners, returned soldiers and casual labourers.

The Arts and Crafts

457 Tasmanian artists of the twentieth century: painters, sculptors, printmakers and photographers 1900-1985.
Sue Backhouse. Hobart: Pandani Press, 1988. 244p. bibliogs.
A landmark directory of all twentieth-century Tasmanian artists. The alphabetically arranged individual entries contain biographical details, exhibitions both individual and selected group, collections in which works are represented, and a select bibliography. Nineteenth-century artists are listed in Joan Kerr's monumental work *The dictionary of Australian artists: painters, sketchers, photographers and engravers to 1870*, published in 1992. The drawback is that the names of artists must be known as the listing is alphabetical and there is no access by the artist's domicile.

458 Tasmanian vision. The art of nineteenth century Tasmania: paintings, drawings and sculpture from European exploration and settlement to 1900.
Hendrik and Julianna Kolenberg. Hobart: Tasmanian Museum and Art Gallery, 1987. 115p. bibliog.
This splendidly illustrated and annotated catalogue represents years of work by the author, who is the Curator of the Tasmanian Art Gallery in Hobart, for the Bicentennial Exhibition in 1988. The catalogue is a permanent and so far the sole comprehensive record of the rich 19th-century art developments in the island.

459 Images in opposition: Australian landscape painting 1801-1890.
Tim Bonyhady. Melbourne: Oxford University Press, 1985. 192p. bibliog.
Tasmania attracted many of the colonial landscape painters. There are textual references to Tasmania throughout the book and painters such as John Glover, W. C. Piguenit and John Skinner are discussed in detail.

460   **Artist in early Australia and their portraits: a guide to the portrait painters of early Australia with special reference to colonial New South Wales and Van Diemen's Land to 1850 with detailed biographies, catalogues of works, and sources of Australian portraiture.**
Eve Buscombe.   Sydney: Eureka Research, 1978. 421p. bibliog.
This scholarly who's who of artists is fully illustrated with more than six hundred photographs of portraits. It is indexed under the names of both artists and subjects. There are separate sections on the artists of Tasmania and New South Wales.

461   **Catalogue of oil paintings from the permanent collection of the Queen Victoria Museum and Art Gallery.**
Barbara Chapman.   Launceston: Queen Victoria Museum and Art Gallery, 1984. 114p.
The collection in the Launceston Queen Victoria Museum and Art Gallery, opened in 1891, is best known for the landscapes of John Glover and the portraits painted by Robert Dowling.

462   **More old Tasmanian prints: a companion volume to *The engravers of Van Diemen's Land* and *Old Tasmanian prints*.**
Clifford Craig.   Launceston: Foot & Playsted, 1983. 389p. bibliog.
This volume brings to a conclusion Dr Craig's monumental task of describing and listing all prints of Tasmanian interest produced from the time of the 18th-century maritime explorers to the eve of Australian federation in 1900. The first volume was entitled *The engravers of Van Diemen's Land* and published in 1961, and the second volume entitled *Old Tasmanian prints: prepared in Great Britain, Europe and on the mainland of Australia* in 1964. All three volumes are generously illustrated with reproductions of the prints. Together they form the standard authority on printed graphic work relating to Tasmania.

463   **Notes on Tasmaniana: a companion volume to *The engravers of Van Diemen's Land*, *Old Tasmanian prints* and *More old Tasmanian prints*.**
Clifford Craig.   Launceston: Foot & Playsted, 1986. 324p. bibliog.
This book was published after the death of Dr Craig, surgeon, historian, author and collector who died in 1986 at the age of 90. It documents in an anecdotal manner the highlights of a collector's career which began in 1938, as well as other interesting aspects of Tasmania. Dr Craig sold the bulk of his large collection of Tasmaniana in 1975 by auction through Christie's (Australia) in Launceston. The catalogue is entitled *The important collection of books, manuscripts, prints, drawings and paintings relating to the discovery and history of Van Diemen's Land and Tasmania . . . the property of Dr Clifford Craig of Launceston, Tasmania.* See also item no. 462.

464   **W. C. Piguenit, 1836-1914: retrospective.**
   Christa E. Johannes, Anthony V. Brown.   Hobart: Tasmanian
   Museum and Art Gallery, 1992. 112p. bibliog.

William Charles Piguenit, 'the first Australian-born artist of note', was born in Hobart
in 1836. After a career as a draughtsman in the Survey Office, Piguenit resigned in
1872 to become a professional landscape painter. He travelled throughout Tasmania
and painted the wild scenery. In 1875 he moved to Sydney. This exhibition catalogue
reproduces many of the artist's paintings and provides much valuable information on
him.

465   **The art of John Glover.**
   John McPhee.   Melbourne: Macmillan, 1980. 102p. bibliog.

The landscape painter John Glover emigrated to Tasmania at the age of 62 in 1829.
For the next twenty years until his death in 1849 he sketched and painted the
Tasmanian landscape in relative isolation. It was not until the late 1950s that Glover
was recognized as the first Australian painter to capture the peculiar qualities of the
Australian bush. His portrayal of gum trees, light and colours was accurate. This book
contains a rich selection of the best of Glover's work, principally that executed in
Tasmania.

466   **Simpkinson de Wesselow: landscape painter in Van Diemen's
   Land and the Port Phillip district 1844-1848.**
   Max Angus.   Hobart: Blubber Head Press, 1984. 191p. bibliog.

Sailor-artist Francis Guillemard Simpkinson de Wesselow was a superb sketcher, who
lived in Hobart from 1844 to 1848. During his stay in Tasmania he produced some
200 drawings and watercolours. Many of these are reproduced in this superb large-
format volume with an accompanying text by Max Angus providing both a biography
of the artist and an evaluation of his work.

467   **Wainewright in Tasmania.**
   Robert Crossland.   Melbourne: Oxford University Press, 1954. 166p.
   bibliog.

Thomas Griffiths Wainewright, artist and writer, was transported for life to Tasmania
for forgery in 1837. Although a convict, he was allowed some liberties, because of
failing health, and so was able to practise his beloved painting. Many of the portraits
he produced at this time are among the best of his works, full of sensitivity and perception. Some twenty-five of these are reproduced in this biography of Wainewright.

468   **Haughton Forrest 1826-1925.**
   George Deas Brown.   Melbourne: Malakoff Fine Arts Press, 1982.
   183p. bibliog.

Haughton Forrest arrived in Tasmania in 1876. After five years in municipal employ-
ment he retired in 1881 and for the rest of his long life devoted himself to art, painting
many fine marine subjects and Tasmanian landscapes. His output was prolific and his
pictures have recently come into vogue again.

469 **Skinner Prout in Australia 1840-48.**
Tony Brown, Hendrik Kolenberg. Hobart: Tasmanian Museum and Art Gallery, 1986. 80p. bibliog.

John Skinner Prout, an English artist, spent the years 1840-48 in Australia. From 1844 to 1848 he lived and painted in Tasmania and made a great impact on the local art scene by means of lectures, exhibitions and his lithographic sets: *Tasmania illustrated*, 2 volumes published in 1844 and 1846 respectivley. Prout painted in the picturesque manner and championed the artist's right to interpret freely rather than merely imitate the scene before him. This catalogue of an exhibition held in Hobart from 9 December 1986 to 1 February 1987, as well as in other locations on the mainland, contains many reproductions of his landscapes.

470 **Thomas Bock: convict engraver, society portraitist.**
Compiled by Diane Dunbar. Launceston: Queen Victoria Museum and Art Gallery, 1991. 107p. bibliogs.

Thomas Bock arrived in Tasmania as a convict in 1824, was pardoned in 1833, and died in 1855. He was the most versatile artist of the period, as he worked in several media, exhibiting a high level of artistic and technical competence in each of them. This catalogue, produced for exhibitions in Launceston and Canberra, is an excellent documentation of Bock's life and his contribution to colonial art.

471 **William Buelow Gould: convict artist of Van Diemen's Land.**
Garry Darby. Sydney: Copperfield Publishing, 1980. 136p. bibliog.

Gould was transported to Tasmania for stealing, and arrived at Hobart Town in 1827 at the age of 26. Until his death in 1853 he painted exquisite watercolours of flowers, birds and fishes, perfect in technical detail. He was a hardened felon, being repeatedly convicted for stealing and drunkenness. After yet another conviction in 1832, Gould was sentenced to Macquarie Harbour; the sketches he made there provide a unique topographical record of the penal settlement. He also painted a few portraits, including some of Aborigines.

472 **Amy Sherwin: the Tasmanian nightingale.**
Judith A. Bowler. Dynwyrne: The Author, 1982. 67p. bibliog.

Amy Sherwin, a brilliant singer, was one of the few Tasmanians who became world famous. This is the story of her rise to fame from a humble homestead in the Huon Valley to the great theatres of Europe and America. The book is well researched and very readable. There are thirty photographs and reproductions of programmes and letters.

473 **A history of the Theatre Royal, Hobart, from 1834.**
Prepared by Michael Roe. Hobart: Law Society of Tasmania, 196-[?]. 48p.

A short memoir of the development of the Theatre Royal, as well as of performers and performances at the Theatre.

474 **Tasmanian photographers 1840-1940: a directory.**
Chris Long. Edited by Gillian Winter.   Hobart: Tasmanian Historical
Research Association and Tasmanian Museum and Art Gallery, 1995.
130p.

This directory contains entries for all known professional and notable amateur photographers and cinematographers (both resident and visiting), working in Tasmania
during the first century after the introduction of photography in the 1840s. It includes
the dates and places of operation and, where possible, additional reference sources, for
more than 700 individuals and studios. The directory contains more than 250 illustrations, including photographers' marks and advertisements as well as representative
images.

475 **Beautiful & useful: the arts and crafts movement in Tasmania.**
Caroline Miley.   Launceston: Queen Victoria Museum and Art
Gallery, 1987. 70p.

A well-researched summary of the movement in Tasmania. Many illustrations enhance
the text.

476 **Early colonial furniture in New South Wales and Van Diemen's
Land.**
Clifford Craig, Kevin Fahy, E. Graeme Robertson.   Melbourne:
Georgian House, 1972. 220p. bibliog.

As in other parts of the British Empire, the designs of early colonial furniture of
Australia were based on those found in England during the same period. This book
examines how English styles were transferred to Australia, discusses the native
timbers used and finally provides a list, with biographies, of cabinet makers, in both
New South Wales and Tasmania. Over 200 photographs depict the majority of the
interesting historical pieces known to the authors.

Architecture

477 Early buildings of southern Tasmania.

E. Graeme Robertson. Melbourne: Georgian House, 1970. 2 vols.

This book is a sequel to the author's *Early houses of Northern Tasmania: an historical and architectural review*, published also in two volumes in 1964. Together, this well-researched work documents in words and photographs the architectural heritage of Tasmania from the 1830s to the 1850s. Some later buildings are also included.

478 Old colonial architecture in New South Wales and Tasmania.

Hardy Wilson. Sydney: Ure Smith, in association with the National Trust of Australia (N.S.W.), 1975. 10p. + 50 plates.

Hardy Wilson, mystic and poet in prose as well as architect, was the first to draw attention, in picture and print, to the beauty of early Australian architecture. In his introduction to this collection of drawings, first published in 1924, he describes some of the journey he made in his search for the early buildings of the colonial era, and discusses the influence of Georgian architecture on that of Australia. He spent his last years in Tasmania captured by 'the spirit of the place'.

479 John Lee Archer: Tasmanian architect and engineer.

Roy Smith. Hobart: Tasmanian Historical Research Association, 1962. 70p. bibliog.

A biography, by a professional architect, of the Irish-born civil engineer and architect, who designed many early colonial structures in Tasmania. The book lists all known works of Archer and reproduces many original drawings from the Tasmanian State Archives as well as photographs of the structures.

480   **The National Trust in Tasmania.**
      Text by J. N. D. Harrison. Photographs by Frank Bolt.   Sydney:
      Cassell, 1980. 239p. bibliog.

A photographic record of a sample of the architectural treasures which are of concern
to the National Trust of Australia in Tasmania.

481   **Mansions, cottages and all saints: residences and churches – the**
      heritage of Greater Hobart, Tasmania.
      Drawings by Audrey Holiday. Text by Walker Eastman.   Hobart:
      Printing Authority of Tasmania, 1994. 182p. bibliog.

The book contains 85 drawings of historic buildings in the Greater Hobart area, with
commentaries by the artist's husband. In 1988 Audrey Holiday, in collaboration with
writer John Trigg, published a collection of 110 drawings entitled *From Black Snake*
to Bronte: heritage buildings of the Derwent Valley in Tasmania, sketches and com-
mentaries (1807-1914).

482   **Early houses of the north west coast of Tasmania.**
      Written and illustrated by Kathleen Cocker.   Western Junction: G. H.
      Stancombe, 1984. 2nd ed. 80p.

A depiction in watercolours of historic houses of the north-west coast of Tasmania.
The National Trust of Australia (Tasmania) sponsored the publication, and the
historical accounts about most of the buildings have been supplied by members of the
Trust in the north-western region. Cocker collaborated with G. Hawley Stancombe to
produce a similar book showing structures from around Tasmania – *Pioneer tapestry:*
buildings of early Tasmania. This book was published in 1977.

483   **An architectural guide to the city of Hobart.**
      Prepared by members of the Royal Australian Institute of Architects,
      Tasmanian Chapter.   Hobart: The Institute, 1984. 56p. maps.

A guide to both historic and modern buildings in Hobart. The booklet is intended for
tourists – after a short introduction on the styles of architecture represented in Hobart,
short descriptions of all buildings included are accompanied by photographs and
detailed locational maps.

484   **Early Tasmanian bridges.**
      Roy Smith.   Launceston: Foot & Playsted, 1969. 107p. maps. bibliog.

The author follows the Midland Highway, connecting Hobart to Launceston, and
describes the history and method of construction of bridges erected in the first half of
the nineteenth century. The book contains a strong heritage message and argues for
preservation.

485 **Ross Bridge and the sculpture of Daniel Herbert.**
Text by Leslie Greener, Norman Laird. Photographs by Norman Laird.
Hobart: Fullers Bookshop, 1971. 192p. bibliogs.

The beautiful bridge at Ross, opened in 1836, with its carvings of icons, can arguably
be claimed to be a work of art. In this book the authors meticulously describe both the
history of the bridge and the meaning of the icons. The achievements of the key
workers, James Colbeck and Daniel Herbert, are discussed in detail.

Sport and Recreation

86 Tasmania's greatest sportsmen.
Neil Kearney.   Launceston: Foot & Playsted, 1977. 86p.
Seventeen sportsmen, who have distinguished themselves in their respective disciplines either nationally or internationally, are featured in this booklet.

87 Island summers: a history of Tasmanian representative cricket.
Ric Finlay.   Hobart: St David's Park Publishing, 1992. 232p.
The story of interstate and international cricket in Tasmania.

88 Boon: in the firing line, an autobiography.
With A. Mark Thomas.   Sydney: Sun, 1993. 161p.
An autobiography by David Boon, Tasmania's best cricketer over the last 18 years, written with the assistance of A. Mark Thomas, sports news editor for the *Examiner* newspaper in Launceston (see item no. 512). Before his recent retirement, Boon represented Australia in Test matches and one-day internationals for over 10 years. He continues to play for Tasmania.

89 A history of Tasmanian cricket.
Roger Page.   Hobart: L. G. Shea, Government Printer, 1957. 143p.
An account of the development of the game in Tasmania from its beginnings in the 1820s to the mid-1950s. Many photographs accompany the text.

90 Prominent Tasmanian cricketers from Marshall to Boon.
Rick Smith.   Launceston: Foot & Playsted, 1985. 298p. bibliog.
The author has selected more than forty Tasmanian cricketers who in his estimation have been the best players of the game over the last 130 years.

491   **50 years of cricket in Tasmania's north east.**
S. G. Chapple.   Launceston: The Author, 1985. 93p.
Written by a local identity who was active in business and public affairs and wh
distinguished himself on the cricket field.

492   **To celebrate a century of Northern Tasmanian cricket: the story of**
the Northern Tasmanian Cricket Association.
Compiled and edited by R. Williams, with assistance from R. Smith.
Launceston: Foot & Playsted, 1986. 143p.
This history was published in 1986 to commemorate one hundred years of th
Northern Tasmanian Cricket Association based in Launceston.

493   **A century of Tasmanian football 1879-1979.**
Ken Pinchin. Edited by Allan Leeson.   Hobart: Tasmanian Football
League, 1979. 192p.
This book deals with the origins and progress of Australian Rules football i
Tasmania, from the time of the establishment of the Tasmanian Football Association
later to become the Tasmanian Football League in 1879. Many black-and-white a
well as colour photographs accompany the text.

494   **From then . . . till now: a historical review of the Tasmanian Turf**
Club, racing identities, racehorses and courses.
W. C. S. Oliver.   Launceston: Tasmanian Turf Club, 1987. 96p.
The author has held many positions in the racing industry for 50 years and writes from
first-hand knowledge and the records of the Tasmanian Turf Club. This book is th
official history of the Club.

495   **Tasmanian trout waters.**
Greg French.   Hobart: 1994. 336p. maps.
A vade-mecum to trout fishing in Tasmania. Every trout water on the island i
discussed in detail. The text is accompanied by maps and many black-and-whit
photographs. A comprehensive guide to trout fishing in the Central Highlands wa
published by Rob Sloane and Guy French in 1991: *Trout guide: a guide to trou*
fishing in Tasmania's Central Highlands.

496   **The great trout of Lake Pedder.**
Ned Terry.   Hobart: Artemis Publishing, 1994. 120p. map.
After many battles with conservationists, the scenic and geologically unique Lak
Pedder was inundated in 1972 by the damming of the Serpentine River. One conse
quence of this controversial action, because of an explosion of the food supply, was
sudden big increase in the average size of the trout in the new Lake Pedder – monster
up to 10 kilograms in weight were not an uncommon catch in the Lake's heyday. Thi
book tells the story of those halcyon days for anglers.

497 **Angling in Australia: its history and writings.**
Bob Dunn. Sydney: David Ell Press, 1991. 320p. bibliog.
A richly illustrated history of recreational fishing in Australia. There are many
references to Tasmania throughout the text, especially with regard to catching trout
and fly fishing.

498 **Fly-fisher in Tasmania: an acquaintance with the trout of the
rivers and lakes of Tasmania, Australia.**
David Scholes. Melbourne: Melbourne University Press, 1961. 208p.
bibliog.
Still one of the classics on Australian fly fishing. The author has fished in Tasmania,
the rest of Australia and the world for over fifty years, and has related his own
experiences and preferred advice to other anglers in numerous books. Some other
Scholes titles recommended for the keen angler are: *Tasmanian angler* (1970); *Trout
days* (1986) and *Fly fishing pictorial* (1990).

499 **Dry-fly fishing for trout.**
Tony Ritchie. Sydney: Kangaroo Press, 1994. 96p. bibliog.
A dry-fly specialist, the author is an authority on his subject. The book is of great
value to the angler visiting Tasmania, where the fly fishing is probably as good
as anywhere in the world. The conditions for fishing here can be unique and
Ritchie imparts the special knowledge required for success. Diagrams and coloured
photographs accompany the text.

500 **More about trout: an appreciation of fly fishing for wild trout.**
Robert Sloane. Hobart: Tas-Trout Publications, 1989. 147p.
This book, and an earlier one *The truth about trout* published in 1983, are valuable
reference works for any angler intending to fly fish in Tasmanian waters.

501 **Paddle about Tasmania: a guide to canoeing, kayaking and rafting
in Tasmania.**
Robert McGuiness, Sandra Gorter, David Masters. Hobart: Tasmanian
Canoe Association, 1984. 100p. maps. bibliog.
A guide to Tasmania's canoeing experiences. More than any other Australian state,
Tasmania is blessed with a magnificent variety of rivers, lakes, estuaries and coast-
lines. Over 90 locations are discussed in detail and maps show how to get there.

502 **A hundred years of yachting.**
Compiled by E. H. Webster, L. Norman. Hobart: The Government of
Tasmania, the Hobart Marine Board and the Hobart City Council,
1936. 256p.
This is an exhaustive history of yachting in Tasmania, which would be much more
useful if an index were provided. The book is crammed with facts but lacks a
connecting theme. It contains no bibliography but many black-and-white photographs
of yachts, natural features and the built environment of Tasmania.

503   **The 50th Sydney–Hobart ocean racing classic: Melbourne–Hobart 1994.**

Richard Bennett. Text by Bob Ross.   Hobart: Richard Bennett, 1995. 96p. map.

The Sydney–Hobart yacht race started in 1945 and has become an annual event and the principal ocean race in Australia. The book commemorates the 50th anniversary race in 1994. It briefly tells the story of the event, but is essentially a colour photographic essay of the yachts at sea. There are many dramatic shots of the wild Tasmanian coast. A similar book, without the professional photographs of Bennett, is *Sydney to Hobart: the 1994 golden commemorative Sydney to Hobart yacht race log*. This book gives a brief history of each of the 50 races.

504   **100 walks in Tasmania.**

Tyrone T. Thomas.   Melbourne: Hill of Content, 1989. 3rd fully rev. ed. 371p.

Spectacular scenery and bushland abound in Tasmania and much of it can be reached only on foot. This book presents 100 of the best walking areas on the island. For safety reasons certain remote places have been omitted. Most routes are circuits and maps are included. Special sections deal with safety, mapping and navigation. The text is accompanied by drawings and colour photographs. Another useful guide for the hiking enthusiast is *Day walks in Tasmania* by Mark Dickenson, Chris Howard and Greg Rubock; it was published in 1993.

505   **The Overland Track: a walkers' notebook.**

Tasmanian Department of Parks, Wildlife and Heritage.   Hobart: The Department, 1992. 80p.

The Overland Track connects the two best-known features of the Cradle Mountain–Lake St Clair National Park. This park is part of the Tasmanian Wilderness World Heritage Area. The handy pocket-sized guide provides information on flora and fauna encountered on the hike, as well as background data on geology and history, and hints on provisions and safety. The walk is 73 km in length, and on the average should take about 5 days to complete.

506   **Cradle Mountain, Lake St Clair and Walls of Jerusalem national parks.**

John Chapman, John Siseman.   Melbourne: Pindari Publications and John Chapman, 1993. 3rd ed. 160p. maps.

The mountains of Central Tasmania offer some of the best hiking country in Australia. This is a spectacular wilderness area, very different from the traditional concept of the Australian bush. The book provides detailed track notes, including maps, and information on all the popular routes, as well as some lesser-known walks into remote country. A very similar guide to another wilderness area is the author's *South West Tasmania: a guidebook for bushwalkers* (3rd ed., 1990).

507   **Family bushwalks in Tasmania's Huon Valley.**
Nell Tyson, Annie Rushton.   Dover: Driftwood Publishing, 1995.
96p. maps.
The hikes listed in this booklet are located in the Huon Valley region, within easy
reach of Hobart. Although primarily intended for families with children, the walks are
recommended for tourists of all ages.

Food and Drink

508 **A food lover's guide to Tasmania.**
Sue Dyson, Roger McShane.   Hobart: The Quill Consultancy, 1992.
179p.
Tasmania is noted for its excellent fruit and vegetables, cheese, seafood and
increasingly, for its fine wines. This is the guide to good eating and drinking in the
island state. The authors have selected and described the state's best restaurants, bakers,
butchers, fishmongers, greengrocers, delicatessens, and food and wine producers. This
is an indispensable companion for the gourmet traveller.

509 **Tasmania.**
In: *Stephanie's Australia: travelling and tasting.*   Stephanie
Alexander. Photographs by John Hay.   Sydney: Allen & Unwin, 1991,
p. 136-161.
Stephanie Alexander is one of Australia's leading chefs and food writers. In 1990 her
restaurant Stephanie's in Melbourne was included as one of the Top Ten restaurants in
the world by the *Courvoisier book of the best*. Here she travels to Tasmania and
describes the gourmet food scene in the island state.

510 **Tasmania.**
In: *Wine atlas of Australia and New Zealand.*   James Halliday.
Sydney: Angus & Robertson, 1991, p. 294-303.
The wine-making industry in Tasmania started in the late 1950s. Many of the wines
have now achieved distinction for their cool-climate characteristics. This chapter
presents an overview of the industry and lists the wineries, with comments on vintages
and the quality of the wines produced. For ratings of vintages and quality of
Tasmanian wines the wine buff may consult annual lists, such as *Australian and New
Zealand wine vintages* by Robin Bradley; *The Penguin good Australian wine guide* by
Mark Shield and Phill Meyer; and *Pocket guide to the wines of Australia and New
Zealand* by James Halliday.

Newspapers, Magazines and Periodicals

511   The Mercury.
> Hobart: Davies Bros., 1854- . daily.

The daily newspaper of the capital city of Tasmania has a circulation of around 53,000 copies and concentrates on local news. The company also publishes the *Sunday Tasmanian*.

512   The Examiner.
> Launceston: Examiner Newspapers P/L, 1900- . daily.

This is the daily newspaper of Tasmania's second-largest city, Launceston. It has a circulation of around 38,000 copies.

513   This week in Tasmania.
> Devonport: Peter Isaacson Publications, 1984- . monthly.

A regular guide to coming events and tourist attractions in Tasmania. Available free to visitors and tourists at points of arrival and at tourist offices.

514   The treasure islander.
> Hobart: Davies Bros., 1984- . monthly.

A large-format, regular colour guide to tourist attractions, providing information of use to the traveller in Tasmania.

515   Island Magazine.
> Hobart: Island Magazine, 1981- .

First appeared under the title *Tasmanian Review* in 1978, changed to *Island Magazine* in 1981 and has been called simply *Island* since 1990. Although the magazine's main preoccupation through the years has been Australian and international literature, it has always carried articles concerned with current issues not only relevant to Australia as a whole but also to Tasmania specifically. Thus, *Island* can be used as a useful source of information on matters that have preoccupied Tasmanians over the last twenty-five years. An index for issues 1–19, up to and including Winter 1984, appeared in issue 20, Spring 1985. A selection of writings from its first ten years of existence was published in 1989; that was entitled *First rights: a decade of Island magazine*, and was edited by Michael Denholm and Andrew Sant.

516   **Tasmanian Historical Research Association. Papers and Proceedings.**
Hobart: Tasmanian Historical Research Association, 1951- . quarterly.

The Association meets monthly, and speakers present formal papers to members on all aspects of Tasmanian history. These are then printed in the *Papers and Proceedings*. The cumulated papers over the last half-century present a rich source of the state's history to the researcher. An index to the first 30 volumes was published by the Association in 1984: *Index to the papers and proceedings, volumes 1-30, 1951-1983*; it was compiled by Margaret Glover.

517   **Bulletin of the Centre for Tasmanian Historical Studies.**
Hobart: Centre for Tasmanian Historical Studies, University of Tasmania, 1985- . annual.

The *Bulletin* is a regular publication of the Centre for Tasmanian Historical Studies within the History Department of the University of Tasmania. The Centre is a body committed to research into and encouragement of the pursuit of Tasmanian historical studies and the *Bulletin* usually contains scholarly historical articles and proceedings of conferences and seminars.

518   **Tasmania: economic insights and outlook.**
Hobart: Department of Treasury and Finance, 1992- . quarterly.

This official quarterly publication provides the only regular, comprehensive analysis of the Tasmanian economy. Each issue contains a special feature which presents an overview of recent developments in a particular segment of the economy. An index to all of these features appears in each issue.

519   **Tasmanian business reporter.**
Hobart: Tasmanian Chamber of Commerce and Industry, 1981- . monthly.

Provides regular news and information on Tasmanian business, including current trends in government activities affecting business, new products, training, industrial relations, marketing, conventions and meetings, and people in business.

520   **The Tasmanian conservationist.**
Hobart: Tasmanian Conservation Trust, 1981- . quarterly.

This is the regular newsletter of the Tasmanian Conservation Trust and provides news and information on environmental issues.

Reference Works

521   **The Australian encyclopaedia.**
Sydney: Australian Geographic Society, 1988. 5th ed. 9 vols.
The latest edition of the *Australian encyclopaedia* consists of some three million
words set out in nine volumes. The first eight volumes constitute the encyclopaedia
proper; the ninth volume comprises a statistical appendix and a comprehensive index,
through which Tasmanian entries can be traced. People and places occur in the
alphabetical sequence. Some fundamental articles in earlier editions, especially the
second published in 1953, retain their intrinsic value.

522   **Cyclopedia of Tasmania: an historical and commercial review;
descriptive and biographical, facts, figures and illustrations. An
epitome of progress: businessmen and commercial interests.**
Hobart: Maitland & Krone, 1900. 2 vols.
This huge work was published 'to supply detailed information in regard to persons,
places, industries etc., not to be found elsewhere.' It is an unequalled reference to
Tasmania as it was at the end of the 19th century. It is useful today as an historical
work. A facsimile edition was published in 1988. A broadly similar volume was
published in 1931 entitled *Cyclopedia of Tasmania: an historical, industrial and
commercial review; biographical facts, showing the progress of Tasmania.*

523   **Tasmanian year book.**
Canberra: Australian Bureau of Statistics, 1967- . Annual until 1986,
then biennial.
'This is the 25th edition. Since its inception the *Year book* has been an invaluable
source of reference information about the State of Tasmania, providing a permanent
record of the economic and social developments of the time. Subjects covered include
Tasmania's physical environment, its history and structure of government, and details
of the wide range of economic and social statistics collected by the Australian Bureau
of Statistics. It is designed to be readily understood by all who wish to acquire a broad
knowledge of the State, as well as those who have a practical use for the statistics.'

More detailed, and in many cases more up-to-date, statistics of the various topics covered may be obtained by reference to the list of related publications included at the end of each chapter.

524 Australian dictionary of biography.
Melbourne: Melbourne University Press, 1966- . 13 vols to date.

The largest and most scholarly source of Australian biographical information is complete to 1939 in 12 volumes. The 13th volume, published in 1993, covers the years 1940-80, A–De. When volumes 13–16 have been completed, work will begin on the period 1981-90. People connected with Tasmania can be looked up only under their surnames. There is an index volume to volumes 1–12, which contains a listing of the names according to the main occupations cited, and another listing under places of birth.

525 Who's who in Australia.
Melbourne: Information Australia Group, 1906- . annual. Latest ed., 32nd, 1996.

Lists prominent Australians with career details, including Tasmanians. The *Australian dictionary of biography* (see item no. 524) lists only people who have died.

526 Australian autobiographical narratives: an annotated bibliography. Volume I: To 1850.
Kay Walsh, Joy Hooton.   Canberra: Australian Scholarly Editions Centre, University College, ADFA and National Library of Australia, 1993. 178p. bibliog.

Tasmanian autobiographies are listed, in the place index under Van Diemen's Land, Hobart, Launceston and smaller localities. There are over fifty autobiographies of Tasmanian interest and they throw much light on the early life of the colony. Summaries of the content of each entry are given. Besides the place index there is also a subject index.

527 The history, politics and economy of Tasmania in the literature 1856-1959.
Elizabeth Flinn.   Hobart: University of Tasmania, 1961. 119p.

This bibliography provides a list of references to books and articles in periodicals and magazines dealing with Tasmania's history, politics and economics which were written in the years between the establishment of self-government in 1856 and 1959.

528 Bass Strait bibliography: a guide to the literature on Bass Strait covering scientific and non-scientific material.
General editors: Stephen Murray-Smith, and John Thompson. Melbourne: Victorian Institute of Marine Science, 1981. 271p.

The state of Tasmania includes many neighbouring islands, principally King and Flinders Islands in Bass Strait. Consequently, much of the material listed in this bibliography relates to Tasmania.

529 **Historical bibliographies of Tasmania.**
Series editor: Richard Ely.   Hobart: Centre for Tasmanian Historical
Studies, University of Tasmania, 1989 to date.

About ten volumes are planned in this series: 'Each volume is designed to assist
inquirers who seek a guide to printed materials relevant to historical developments in
a particular region of Tasmania during [mainly] the last two centuries. Commentaries
are added to listed items, briefly indicating their character and suggesting specific
ways in which such items may be helpful both to the serious historical investigator
and to those simply wishing to learn more about the history of a particular area.' So
far, *The history of the Huon, Channel, Bruny Island region: printed sources* by
Richard Ely, *History of the Midlands–Central Plateau region: printed sources*, and
History of West and South-West Tasmania: a guide to printed sources – the latter two
both by Tim Jetson – have been published. Another three volumes are in preparation.

530 **Index to the Papers and Proceedings: volumes 1-30, 1951-1983.**
Compiler: Anne Rand. General editor: Margaret Glover.   Hobart:
Tasmanian Historical Research Association, 1991. 199p.

This is the key to a valuable body of research material in Tasmanian history. It is an
author, subject and title index, with a particular emphasis on the listing of authors and
titles of papers presented to the meetings of the Tasmanian Historical Research
Association. The index is an indispensable research tool for the study of Tasmanian
history.

531 **Shipping arrivals and departures, Tasmania. Volume I: 1803-1833.
Parts I, II and III.**
Ian Hawkins Nicholson.   Canberra: Roebuck, 1983. 223 + 94p. maps.
(Roebuck Society Publication, no. 30).

'The primary purpose of this publication is to provide the fullest possible record of
shipping movements in and out of Tasmanian ports, particularly for Hobart and
Launceston, from the beginning of settlement in 1803 to the end of 1833. Also
included in the list, in sequence of occurrence, are other reports and events of a
nautical nature, so the book is a chronicle of maritime history for the first 31 years of
the colony of Van Diemen's Land.' The chronicle is continued by Nicholson in
Roebuck Society Publication no. 33, published in 1985 with the title *Shipping arrivals
and departures, Tasmania. Volume II: 1834-1842 (Parts I, II and III) and Gazetteer of
Tasmanian shipping 1803-1842 (Part IV)*. A third volume by Graeme Broxam is in
preparation and will cover the period 1843-1850.

532 **Checklists of Royal Commissions, Select Committees of Parliament
and Boards of Inquiry. Part II Tasmania 1856-1959.**
D. H. Borchardt.   Sydney: Wentworth Press, 1960. 34p.

An index to public tribunals of inquiry from the establishment of responsible government in 1856 to 1959. A description giving reasons for the establishment of the
inquiry, its conclusions and recommendations accompany each entry. This is an
indispensable tool for anyone researching the development of law and society in
Tasmania. If the reports were printed in the Tasmanian parliamentary papers series,
the reference is given. In 1986, an update was published entitled *Checklist of Royal
Commissions, Select Committees of Parliament and Boards of Inquiry: Commonwealth,*

New South Wales, Queensland, Tasmania and Victoria 1960-1980 and South Australia 1970-1980. This was published by the La Trobe University as its Library Publication no. 30.

533 The guide to government publications in Australia.

Michel Harrington.   Canberra: Australian Government Publishing Service, 1990. 164p. bibliog.

Covers the Commonwealth and the State and Territory governments. Treatment is in chapters by the main series of publications. Tasmanian series can be traced through the index.

534 The government who's who of Australia.

Sydney: Riddell Information Services, 1995- . 3 times a year. Latest ed., 3rd, October 1995.

The Tasmanian sections contain up-to-date listings and descriptions and personnel details of the state government and its executive departments, statutory authorities and local government agencies.

535 Press radio & TV guide: Australia, New Zealand, Pacific Islands.

Edited by Jennifer Peden.   Sydney: Media Monitors Australia, 1914- . Latest ed., 32nd, 1995.

The Tasmanian sections are easily found through the list of contents in this comprehensive media reference guide. A more frequent publication containing similar information in more detail is *Margaret Gee's Australian media guide* which is revised and updated every four months.

536 Tasmania: business & street directory.

Melbourne: Universal Business Directories of Australia, 1950- . irregular. Latest ed., 42nd, 1993.

This very useful publication contains classified listings of businesses in each area of Tasmania entered in the directory. There are 21 areas covering the entire State. Up-to-date summaries of business and industry, tourist attractions and street maps of all major towns are included.

537 Local & family history sources in Tasmania.

Edited by Anne M. Bartlett.   Launceston: Genealogical Society of Tasmania, Inc., 1994. 2nd ed. 119p. maps. bibliog.

The purpose of this book is to provide a survey of the records relating to family history, local history, social history and biography available in Tasmania and to give their lcoation and the means of gaining access to them. In effect, it is a directory of archives, repositories, libraries, museums, historical societies and cemeteries, with detailed descriptions of their holdings. There is also an extensive bibliography.

Indexes

There follow three separate indexes: authors; titles; and subjects. The numbers refer to bibliographical entries and not to pages. Individual index entries are arranged in alphabetical sequence.

Index of Authors

Index of Titles

A

Aboriginal man and
environment in
Australia 200

Aboriginal people of
Tasmania 191

Aboriginal Tasmanians
194

Aboriginal tribes of
Australia . . . 201

Aborigines of Tasmania
193

Account of a voyage to
establish a settlement in
Bass Strait 98

Adventure Bay:
a convenient and safe
place 211

Advocate 387

Affirming flame:
adventures in
continuing education
415

Alexander Pearce of
Macquarie Harbour:
convict – bushranger –
cannibal 188

Allport Library and
Museum of Fine Arts
427

Alpine wildflowers of
Tasmania 80

Among the carrion crows
278

Amy Sherwin: the
Tasmanian nightingale
472

And wealth for toil:
a history of northwest
and western Tasmania
1825-1900 136

Andrew Bent and the
freedom of the press in
Van Diemen's Land
105

Anglican Church in
Tasmania: a diocesan
history to mark the
sesquicentenary 1992
216

Angling in Australia: its
history and writings 497

Annotated bibliography of
the Tasmanian
Aborigines 205

Annotated bibliography of
the Tasmanian
Aborigines 1970-1987
205

Anthology of short stories,
articles and poems by
Tasmanian authors 439

Architectural guide to the
city of Hobart 483

Around Circular Head 137

Art of John Glover 465

Artists in early Australia
and their portraits 460

As the river flows 135

Aspects of Tasmanian
botany: a tribute to
Winifred Curtis 86

Atlas of the Australian
people – 1991 Census:
national overview 245

Atlas of the Australian
people: Tasmania, 1986
Census 245

Atlas of Tasmania 14

Australian and New
Zealand wine vintages
510

Australian
autobiographical
narratives 526

Australian climate
patterns 10

Australian dictionary of
biography 524-5

Australian encyclopaedia
521

Australian Law Reports
290

Australian legal history
283

Australian literature: from
its beginnings to 1935
434

Australian monetary
system 1851 to 1914
301

Australian Newsprint
Mills Limited 1938-1988
324

B

Backsight: a history of
surveying in Tasmania
24

Baptists in Van Diemen's
Land: the story of
Tasmania's first Baptist
church 229

Bartley of 'Kerry Lodge':
a portrait of a pioneer
in Van Diemen's Land
164

Bass Strait: Australia's
last frontier 9

Bass Strait bibliography
528

Bass Strait ketches 367

Battle for the Franklin:
conversations with the
combatants 408

Baudin expedition and the
Tasmanian Aborigines
1802 198

Beautiful & useful: the
arts and crafts
movement in Tasmania
475

Beyond the ramparts: a
bicentennial history of
Circular Head 138

Index of Subjects

man
  influence on the
    environment 100,
    146, 382-3
manufacturing industries
  history 308
mapping
  history 24
maps and atlases 13-16
  Aboriginal tribes 201
  bibliographies 15-16
  canoeing 501
  discovery and
    exploration 18, 22,
    145
  hiking 504-7
  Hobart 116
  roads 536
  south-west Tasmania
    145
  trout fishing 495
Maria Island
  history 156, 174, 181
marine accidents
  history 371-3
Marine Board of Burnie
  360
Marine Board of Hobart
  357
Marine Board of
  Launceston 358
maritime history 364,
  531
maritime studies 423
Martin, John 1812-1875
  178
Meagher, Thomas Francis
  1823-1867 178
Mechanics' Institutes
  history 418
media
  directories 535
media corporations
  history 311
medical policy
  Hobart 256
  Launceston 256
medical practitioners
  biographies 96
medicine
  history 255
Melville, Henry
  1799-1873 104

mental health
  19th century 223
Meredith, Louisa Anne
  1812-1895 54
merino sheep 334
Mersey General Hospital
  history 252
Mersey Valley
  farming 330
Methodist Church
  history 228
Midlands Agricultural
  Association 339
military history 298
military service
  history 298
Miller, Edmund Morris
  1881-1964 421, 434
minerals
  collecting 384
minerals and mining
  11,139, 321
  economic aspects 321
  environmental aspects
    321, 413
  north-west Tasmania 139
  Port Arthur 388
  West Coast 142-3, 353,
    382, 385-7
miners
  strikes 375
missions
  Aborigines 231
  Bass Strait 231
Mitchel, John 1815-1875
  178-9
molluscs 60
monetary policy 301
money
  history 301, 304
Mormons 233
mountains 12
mounted police
  history 292
Mt Lyell Mining and
  Railway Company
  143, 385, 413
museums
  directories 33
music conservatories
  history 426
music education 426
muttonbirding 137, 155

N

national parks 397-8
  hiking 505-6
National Trust of Australia
  (Tasmania) 480
natural history 51, 53-4,
  57
  Flinders Island 32
  Furneaux Group 32
  King Island 31
  Macquarie Island 56,
    158
  south-west Tasmania
    52, 55, 395
natural monuments 39
natural resources
  bibliographies 380
  Central Plateau 383
  conservation 263, 315,
    382, 392-3, 395-6,
    402-5, 407-12
  surveys 380
  Tasman Peninsula 381
naturalists
  biographies 54
New Norfolk
  psychiatric hospitals
    253
new products 309
newspaper proprietors
  biographies 162
newspapers 105, 311, 433
  directories 535
  Hobart 511
  Launceston 162, 165,
    512
newsprint industry
  history 324
Nixon, Anna Maria
  correspondence 218
Nixon, Francis Russell
  1803-1879 218
north-east Tasmania
  cricket 491
  history 131-2, 135, 329
  social life and customs
    329
north-west Tasmania
  history 133, 136-9, 340
  mining 139
Northern Club
  history 243

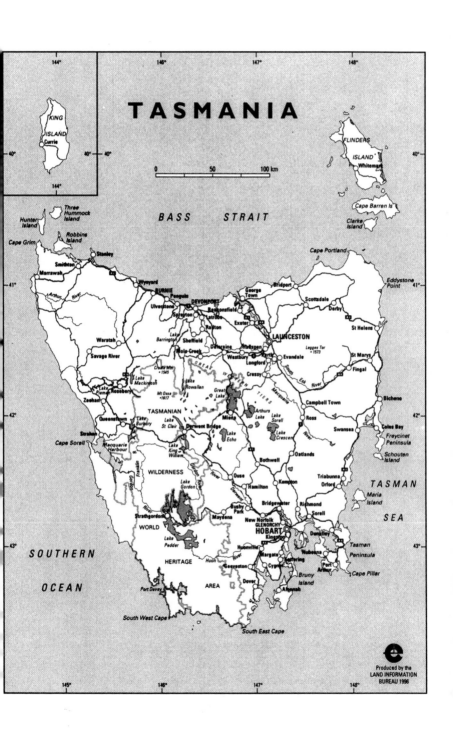

TASMANIA

ALSO FROM CLIO PRESS

INTERNATIONAL ORGANIZATIONS SERIES

Each volume in the International Organizations Series is either devoted to one specific organization, or to a number of different organizations operating in a particular region, or engaged in a specific field of activity. The scope of the series is wide-ranging and includes intergovernmental organizations, international non-governmental organizations, and national bodies dealing with international issues. The series is aimed mainly at the English-speaker and each volume provides a selective, annotated, critical bibliography of the organization, or organizations, concerned. The bibliographies cover books, articles, pamphlets, directories, databases and theses and, wherever possible, attention is focused on material about the organizations rather than on the organizations' own publications. Notwithstanding this, the most important official publications, and guides to those publications, will be included. The views expressed in individual volumes, however, are not necessarily those of the publishers.

VOLUMES IN THE SERIES